# a girl's guide to college

# a girl's guide to college

## making the most of the best four years of your life

traci maynigo

### rabbit's foot press™

A division of Blue Mountain Arts, Inc.
Boulder, Colorado

Library of Congress Catalog Card Number: 2003010119
ISBN-13: 978-1-58786-012-6
ISBN-10: 1-58786-012-0

Certain trademarks are used under license.

Printed in the United States of America.
Fourth Printing: 2006

✪ This book is printed on recycled paper.

This book is printed on fine quality, laid embossed, 80 lb. paper. This paper has been specially produced to be acid free (neutral pH) and contains no groundwood or unbleached pulp. It conforms with all the requirements of the American National Standards Institute, Inc., so as to ensure that this book will last and be enjoyed by future generations.

Library of Congress Cataloging-in-Publication Data

Maynigo, Traci, 1981-
    a girl's guide to college: making the most of the best four years of your life / Traci Maynigo.
        p. cm.
    ISBN 1-58786-012-0 (softcover : alk. paper)
    1. College student orientation—United States. 2. Women college students—United States—Life skills guides. I. Title.

LB2343.32.M325 2003
378.1'982—dc21
                                                                        2003010119
                                                                        CIP

# Blue Mountain Arts, Inc.

P.O. Box 4549, Boulder, Colorado 80306

*This book is dedicated to my grandfather
and grandmother, Raul and Pacita
Manglapus, who have always inspired me to
make a positive difference in people's lives,
even if it is in the smallest way. Lolo and
Mama Pacing, this is my first step.
I love you both.*

# table of contents

# well, it's about time, isn't it?

**Y**ou've spent eighteen years prepping yourself for what will supposedly be "The Best Four Years of Your Life," and now that you're about to enter this other dimension, you're twitching with nervousness and excitement. You've probably heard it before: college isn't easy. In fact, it'll seem almost impossible at times. Of course, the last eighteen years probably weren't quite so easy either. It seems like just yesterday you were throwing animal crackers at your baby brother's face just to get your mom's attention. Soon after that, you were horrified at the sight of your school picture—your braces made your face look like the bumper of the family Volkswagen. Then it was the anguish of adolescence that tormented you: you were dismayed when you got your period, you wished your boobs would grow faster (or at least *evenly*), and boys began to confuse you, giving you that funny feeling inside. Finally, high school came along and you hated the world and all of its confining rules, you wished someone would just *try to understand you.*

Yes, it's fair to say, you've been through a lot, and you're about to endure a heck of a lot more. College is tough, but in a *different* way. You'll get the independence you've been longing for, but you'll have to get used to all the responsibility it entails. But remember, as challenging as college is, it will also be four thrilling and unparalleled years that you'll want to relive forever after. It's the only time in your life when you'll be in a community with thousands of people just as young, confused and energized as you are. You'll learn from each other and share all sorts of experiences. And it's in this environment that you will discover yourself—who you are now, and who you want to become. Plus, of course, there will be parties, new people, and a broad menu of guys to choose from for your own dating pleasure (who could forget *that?*).

Now, with all this beautiful madness to participate in, and all this self-discovery to do, why would you want to fret over stuff like laundry, money, and classes? Well, because college wouldn't be college without it. And the *best* things in life come only with a little bit of suffering.

So, girls: get excited. One thing's for sure, you're going to *love* college.

# getting ready: the summer before college

**W**hen the school year starts, you will enter an entirely new chapter of your life. In a way, it's like starting over completely—a rebirth. You're moving to a new place, and an environment probably much different from your hometown or city. You will be among strangers at first, and soon many of them will form your new circle of friends and your family away from home. Not only will you need to learn to adjust to a new place and new people, but also to the possibly very new stresses of college life. It's a juggling act. You're tossing up classes, activities, friends, work, and dating all at the same time. It's going to take a while to learn to manage them all without letting any one thing (or yourself, for that matter) fall to the floor. Sure, you may have juggled all of these things in high school, but the stakes change once you are experiencing them in the college context. It may seem like it would be impossible to prepare yourself for all of this. And, for the most part, you can't. There are some things you can only learn from experience.

But, knowing that you are about to cross a new threshold, and that you are about to change tremendously as a person, you can think of this summer as the last summer in which you can experience the best of the you that you are now. There's no telling what will happen next, so you might as well just relax, have fun, and **go nuts**. This is your last summer before college. Live it up, girl!

**Go crazy with your friends.** Believe it or not, as the next four years go by—and as you and all your friends get in the habit of doing your own things during the summer—you may be seeing less and less of them. Take some risks this summer, and get your friends to join you.

Don't paste yourself to the television screen and waste away these irreplaceable summer days. Do something different. Remember, these are the people you grew up with; they made you who you are. Show them love and make this last summer a memorable one. And while you're at it, take lots of pictures to hang up on your dorm room wall as reminders of home.

## Do something different, crazy, stupid, or silly this summer!

Go on a road trip with your girlfriends. Have a sleepover for old time's sake. Skydive or bungee jump. Hit the hottest dance clubs downtown and groove till your feet hurt. Check out the hot surfers at the beach. Watch a rock concert. Go camping or fishing. Ride all the roller coasters at an amusement park.

If you've got some unresolved issues with any friends, now's the time to resolve them. Don't worry, they're probably just as ready as you are to patch things up. As you start this new experience and form new relationships, you want to feel secure about your relationships at home. You don't want to be going off to college with emotional baggage (heck, you'll already have enough boxes to carry). Wipe the slate clean.

**Don't forget your family!** As much as you'd like to deny it now, you will really miss them once you're at school. Homesickness will hit you over the head once in a while and you may find yourself calling home more often than the obligatory weekly Sunday calls you initially agree to. So, hit a movie with your little sister or brother, have a heart-to-heart with your mom, organize a family barbecue. Your mom's nagging, your dad's corny jokes, and your brother's farting armpit noises probably aren't so endearing to you now, but secretly, you love them, and you'll love them even more when you're away from them. You'll be wishing you had spent more time with them when you had the chance.

**Break up with your high school boyfriend.** This advice sucks, and no one wants to follow it, but in retrospect, everyone always regrets that they didn't. **Long-distance relationships are unfulfilling and emotionally**

draining. They hold you back and keep you from meeting new people and growing as a person. As much as you might be secure in your relationship, you will soon find that holding on will cause more pain than pleasure. And, as I've said, you will inevitably change. And so will he. It's likely the two people you and he become won't be as compatible as you were in high school. And hey, if you two are in fact meant to be, then you'll be—eventually. **But come to college unrestrained and unattached.** You'll be much happier feeling free to do as you please as you become comfortable with your independence. Also, it might be a good idea to have this break-up well before your departure. Many people choose a policy of *"Once I leave, we're broken up,"* but this might add an unnecessary level of emotional trauma to the already crazy experience of the first days of college.

---

*"For me, the summer between high school and college stretched into an entire year. I had already been accepted into the college I wanted to go to, and I didn't feel ready to be introduced to an entirely new environment that would be my home for the next four years. So I took a year off and went on a cultural study program in Greece for a semester, and then went backpacking around Europe for the second half of the year. Spending this time gave me some rest time and let me get to know and become more comfortable with myself so I could go to college more secure in who I am, and more relaxed about silly things like those little A's, B's, and C's that go at the top of your papers. For some people, and I'm one of them, high school was tense, and I forgot that grades don't run your life. Whether you take a year or just a summer off between high school and college, you have to relax during it and get to know yourself as someone separate from your grades, your friends and your family (as much as you might love all three of those). That way, when you get to college, you're ready for and able to deal with the stress it brings!"*

— Becca Crawford, Oberlin, Ohio

## Give yourself some alone time.

Go on a walk. Go shopping. Read a book. Start writing in a journal. Paint your fingernails and toenails. Take a bubble bath. Learn yoga. Lift weights. Go on a bike ride. Get a massage.

**Get comfortable with yourself and with being independent.** There's more to that than doing your own laundry and cooking your own food. Start managing your money and depending less on your parents. Learn to take care of yourself, even if it's as simple as making your own dentist appointment or buying milk from the grocery store when you've just finished the last carton. The sooner you get comfortable with being self-sufficient, the easier it will be to handle the pressures of college life. And as you become independent in these practical matters, become independent in other ways as well. **Get to know yourself as someone separate from the people in your life, the high school you went to, your GPA, or your score on the SATs.** Keep this in mind: **With all the changes that will be going on in your life in the next four years, the one thing that will always remain constant is yourself.** It is you who will always be there, so value yourself. **Give yourself some alone time.** See what it's like to be without other people. This time for yourself won't necessarily reveal to you anything spectacular about your purpose in life, but it isn't meant to. You'll have lots of time in college (and the rest of your life, for that matter) to discover who you are. Just use this time to appreciate who you are now, regardless of the people or things surrounding you.

## Write a letter to yourself to be opened either at the end of freshman year, or at the end of college.

This is a great exercise in getting to know yourself and your priorities.

**Sort 'em:**

1. SORT your clothes: Separate into dark colors, light colors, and whites. Within each of these categories, separate: delicates, heavily-soiled, towels (and other lint-producing fabrics).
2. Empty all pockets, turn jeans inside out (prevents quick fading), and close zippers, snaps, hooks.
3. Pretreat stains—that is, rub detergent directly on stains.
4. READ ALL LABELS and follow the instructions. DON'T wash something that's "dry clean only."

**Throw 'em in:**

1. Choose the temperature and cycle settings. In general: HOT = whites and heavily soiled clothes; COLD = dark colors and colors that bleed; WARM = everything else. If you're not sure about the temperature for a certain article, read the label.
2. Turn on the machine to fill it with water.
3. Add detergent (DON'T FORGET! I know a few people who have) following the measuring instructions on the package.
4. Throw in your clothes. Don't overload the machine; leave room for the clothes to circulate.

**Dry 'em:**

1. Remove your clothes from the machine as soon as they're done so they won't wrinkle.
2. Separate hang-dry clothes from machine-dry clothes.
3. Set your dryer cycle for WARM for normal clothes, and HOT for sturdier articles like sheets and towels.
4. Throw in a fabric softener sheet, turn on the machine and let it whirl.

**Learn to cook and do laundry while Mom's still around.** Learn some simple recipes from family and friends, or experiment on your own (try to refrain from burning Mom's pots and pans, though). As for laundry, if you already know how, you're much better off than I was. Laundry is honestly going to be such an enormous pain. It's better to learn how to do it before you sacrifice your favorite jeans and tops to trial and error. Perhaps Mom has some stain-lifting secrets to share.

## A few more tips on doing laundry in college:

1. Save your quarters for doing laundry. Keep a jar full of them.
2. Stay with your clothes while they are in the washer and dryer if you can. Bring some studying to do. Believe it or not, your clothes could get stolen, or at least taken out and thrown on a dirty counter, or worse, on the floor. If you can't stay, take note of how long the cycle will take, and make sure you come back a couple of minutes before it ends.
3. Don't leave your laundry basket or detergent lying around unattended. They could get taken, or someone could "borrow" them.
4. Do your laundry when no one else does. During the week and early in the day are good. Weekends tend to be busy.
5. Do your laundry on a regular schedule. Pick a day and time every week or every other week, and make sure you stick to it.

**Get a summer job.** You'll need the money, *trust me.* You should definitely work during the school year (if not to go towards tuition, then for spending money), but it's not something you'll want to think about immediately when you're trying to get settled. Plus you'll want some money to blow off this summer, and also for partying as soon as you get to school. Work somewhere where you've never worked before. *And don't worry about getting a job that will look pretty on your resume.* Get a job that's neither too stressful nor too boring, and that will allow you to work flexible hours. Remember, also, that if you're lucky enough to have your parents help you foot the bill for your college education, your summer job is essentially just for some spending money, so you don't have to work a lot, and you don't have to get paid a lot either. Whatever you do, make sure you leave yourself some time to chill with friends and family, and prepare for school. If you can afford to do so, tell your boss ahead of time that you'll be taking a week or two off at some point.

> **Get a job that's not stressful or boring, and will allow you to work flexible hours and spend time with your friends.**

Try waitressing or hostessing (free food!), or working at a clothing store (discounts!). House-sit, pet-sit, or baby-sit. Deliver pizza. Scoop ice cream. Work as a lifeguard or a cashier. Work for a temp agency or a daycare center.

**Learn about your school.** Find out what it has to offer. Go online and check out its website. Don't just find out about classes, but also about options for extracurricular activities, and about the surrounding area. Talk to current students. If you know someone who either goes there or graduated recently, give him or her a call. Ask that person questions that the website and the campus tour guide won't be able to answer, like where you should hang out, and what dining hall entrées to avoid. Getting to know your new home a little bit beforehand will pay off when you get there. You'll be able to spend more time meeting new people while most of your classmates will still be frantically trying to find their way to the main dining hall. That said, don't stress too much about your preliminary fact-finding because your expectations and plans will be eradicated soon after you get to school. Just get a general idea, and then leave the rest to be found out when you get there. It's more fun that way, anyway.

**Start an exercise plan!** You've got to prepare your body for the freshman fifteen, and now's the time to do it. Not only will you be getting in shape to make room for a few extra pounds, but you'll also get into the habit of working out so that you'll continue to do so once you get to school.

*"For some, going off to college might mean a welcome break from parental supervision and an entry into newfound independence. For others, there will be a realization that this independence means forging out a new life, creating a new home and building new roots because those you have are too far away (or feel too far away) to return to constantly. Right before leaving for college I was sick of what I felt was parochialism in my society, was annoyed with what I deemed to be parental overprotectiveness, and generally ready to leave everything behind. Yet, in spite of these temporary feelings, I found (not too late) that I didn't want to leave with this edge of annoyance and intolerance tainting my memories of the only home I have known, and so I came to terms with what I knew had been good to me. In building the new life I now have, I realize how good the home I left for college was, and how much I still carry around with me wherever I go. I'm glad I realized that, and now, I return home with excitement and an uplifted heart."*

– Joy Chia, Singapore

# chapter two

# packing up:
# getting there with what you need

**a**ll right, girls, the end of the summer is near, and as much as you would love to keep putting it off, it's time to start packing. Unfortunately, it's just not physically possible to transport everything in your room at home directly to your dorm room in one fell swoop, *sans*-boxes, *sans*-mess, *sans*-hassle. But (sigh) as I said earlier, the best things only come with just a little bit of suffering. I like to think of packing as an opportunity to refurbish my wardrobe. As I carefully select what to pack and what not to pack, I realize that with every article I leave behind, I'm opening up a door for a new one later on. And lord *knows* I love to buy new clothes.

So, when it comes to selecting from your current wardrobe, **be a minimalist. Only bring what you know you will use.** This is your chance to rummage through your closet and get rid of every skirt, top, and pair of jeans that you thought you would wear again but never did. If you haven't worn it in the past six months, you won't ever wear it. So don't bring it. In fact, consider getting rid of it altogether. Take it to a thrift shop, or give it to a friend who might actually wear it.

**Just keep it simple.** Less really is more in this case, because who knows how much room you'll have in your closet and dresser. Plus, you'll be moving around so often (at least twice a year), that you'll be grateful to have fewer boxes to lug. You may be tempted to bring *everything*. Trust me, you won't even use half of it. **The same goes for shoes.** Yes, every girl loves her shoes. And you feel like you need to have every pair: the boots, the sandals, the three-inch heels, the two-inch heels ... *Shoes are heavy.* Only bring the essentials.

Feel free to reinvent your wardrobe, but don't stray too far from what you're comfortable wearing. After all, you want your classmates to get to know the authentic you, even if it is the authentic you with a little bit of added panache. You may be having flashbacks to the first day of school every September in your middle or high school years (not too long ago, though it may seem so), when you spent two hours trying on outfits the night before. You wanted to wear something new and different, so that somehow you would seem like a new and different person to these kids who had known you since you were eating glue and crayons. Well, this time around, **you'll be new and different to everyone you meet, no matter what you're wearing, so don't worry too much about it.**

Remember: unless you're going to college on an oil rig in the mid-Atlantic, there will be places to shop for clothes not too far from campus. So, if you discover you are in dire need of a jean skirt just like the one you left hanging in your closet at home, you can buy a new one. And, if you don't ever feel a need for it, then, hey, that was one less thing you had to pack.

**You may be better off waiting to buy any new clothes you want or need until you get to school, so you can get a sense of what people are wearing.**

Then you can decide if you want to sport the standard look, or veer away from the norm. If comfort is your priority, bring what you need, and buy what you're comfortable wearing. If looking good and standing out among your peers are your main concerns, peruse the current trends when you get to school so you can eventually turn some heads and start some trends of your own.

**Remember where you're going and what the weather is like.** The weather may be frigid or it may be sweltering, or it may be somewhere in between. Pack accordingly. Or, even better, wait till you get there, get a feel for what it's like, and *shop* accordingly.

**Try not to pack clothes that are hard to take care of.** This includes clothes that require dry cleaning, hand washing, and ironing. Given the rapid pace of your college life, you will not want to take much time for this sort of tedious task.

I've given you some basic pointers for packing strategies, but ultimately it comes down to you, and what you know you need to bring. However, there are a few things for your closet that you shouldn't forget to pack:

**Socks and underwear.** Pack every pair you have. Buy them in bulk and shove them into every crevice of your suitcase. You'll soon find that as laundry becomes the last thing on your priority list (particularly during paper-writing stress or exam time), you'll appreciate the fact that you're wearing clean underwear and socks under your dirty clothes, making studying and paper-writing that much more comfortable.

**Sweatpants, sweatshirts, T-shirts.** Comfort is key, which is why I recommend sporting the sweatpants-sweatshirt combination when in stress-mode. Bring a couple of pairs of sweatpants and a couple of sweatshirts, with a couple of your favorite T-shirts or tank-tops to wear underneath. Study in your sweats, crash for a power nap in your sweats, then head over to take your exam in your sweats.

**Flip-flops.** These you will need to wear in the shower, for sure, but they are also convenient to slip on when the weather is warm and when you are in a rush to get somewhere (like a 9 a.m. class that you are constantly late for). Get a pair of black ones that you can wear with jeans, pants, a skirt or a sundress.

**Your prom dress.** (Or some kind of formal dress that you would consider wearing again.) You actually *will* get to wear your prom dress more than just once! You will most likely have opportunities to attend formals or semi-formals, whether they are fraternity or sorority formals, or school-sponsored balls or dances. Even if you don't end up using your dress, someone else might be able to, and in return, if you decide you'd rather eat wood than wear that dress again, you'll certainly be able to borrow another one from your roommate or friends. One thing's for sure, you won't want to spend money on a formal dress, so wearing an old one or borrowing someone else's is your best bet.

**Sneakers.** Now, this doesn't mean that you have to part with your leather boots with the three-inch heels. I'd never suggest that you make such a sacrifice. I will point out, however, that racing from class to class from opposite ends of the campus in platforms will leave your heels and toes quite unhappy. Sneakers are just more comfortable. Plus, you'll need them for your regular workouts.

**Hangers.** Don't forget to include the kinds meant for hanging pants and skirts, and padded ones to prevent shoulder nubbies in knit tops.

**Raincoat and umbrella.** In most cases, you won't have the shelter of a car to transport you high and dry from class to class on rainy days. You don't want to be sitting through a boring lecture in rain-soaked, heavy jeans, your feet in a puddle.

**Rollerblades.** If you don't have a pair, consider buying them. They can get you to class much faster and are less of a hassle than bikes. Also, rollerblading is great exercise and a good excuse to take a break from studying.

**Theme outfits.** Especially a Hawaiian shirt or outfit of some sort. You will have the option of attending various fraternity or sorority parties, house parties, and dances that have some sort of theme for which you will want to sport the right outfit. Aside from the Hawaiian theme party, there's also the toga party (bring an old white sheet that you can cut and expose to beer spillage and other such party fouls), the '80s dance (think leg warmers, stretch pants, off-the-shoulder T-shirts), and the '60s and '70s theme dances (hit a thrift store or Mom's closet for some flashy bellbottoms if you don't already own a pair). You can no doubt find outfits for any of these at a thrift store. And if it so happens that parties of said themes don't exist at your school, throw one of your own! It's a great way to meet people and make use of your funky ensembles.

**A big, comfy bathrobe.** Remember, comfort. You can wear this lounging in your room, to and from the bathroom, to a sleepover theme party, or you can use it to keep toasty warm when your heater breaks down.

**Swimsuit.** Swimming makes for a relaxing and fun workout, and if you are going to school by the beach, you want to be well-equipped for bumming on the shore and luring local hotties in from the waves.

When it comes to toiletries and cosmetics, I'll say it again, **only bring what you know you will use.** However, for items that you normally go through quickly and in large amounts, like dental floss or soap, you might consider buying a bunch at home and storing them in a closet or under your bed at school. This will decrease the number of trips you have to make to the drugstore when you are busy with college life. As you choose from the stuff that clutters your bathroom sink and drawers, use this list as a guide:

## For first aid or illness:

☐ First-aid kit
☐ Adhesive bandages
☐ Cough drops
☐ Antacid for heartburn

☐ Pain reliever, such as ibuprofen
☐ Cold medicine
☐ Tissues

## For face:

☐ Tweezers
☐ Toner
☐ Small washcloths

☐ Face wash
☐ Moisturizer
☐ Makeup (try glitter makeup if you don't use it already, it's great for parties and dances)

## For body:

- ☐ Deodorant or antiperspirant
- ☐ Lotion
- ☐ Soap dish (preferably a plastic one with a cover)
- ☐ Towels (lots of them! And make sure they look different, or put your name on them.)
- ☐ Perfume
- ☐ Soap or shower gel
- ☐ Loofah
- ☐ Tampons and/or pads
- ☐ Shaving cream and razor, or hair remover, or waxing kit

## For hair:

- ☐ Hair dryer
- ☐ Hair brush or comb
- ☐ Shampoo & conditioner
- ☐ Styling products

## For teeth:

- ☐ Toothbrush & toothpaste
- ☐ Small cup (for gargling)
- ☐ Floss
- ☐ Mouthwash

## For hands:

- ☐ Nail clipper
- ☐ Nail polish
- ☐ Nail file
- ☐ Nail polish remover

## One more thing:

- ☐ A shower caddy, basket, or bucket of some sort to transport your toiletries to and from the bathroom

You can always buy school supplies when you get to school, but your only option as a resource might be the school's bookstore, which most likely will charge you three times as much as any store in your hometown. So here's a list of supplies you could get ahead of time, as well as some other random things you might forget.

## For school:

- [ ] Rubber bands
- [ ] Permanent markers
- [ ] Paper clips
- [ ] Scissors
- [ ] Index cards
- [ ] Highlighters
- [ ] Pencil sharpener
- [ ] Glue stick or rubber cement
- [ ] Correction fluid
- [ ] Stapler and staples
- [ ] Sticky notes

## For reference:

- [ ] Dictionary
- [ ] Grammar guide
- [ ] The Bible (for religious use or literary reference)
- [ ] Thesaurus
- [ ] A book of quotations
- [ ] Style guide (i.e., *Chicago Manual of Style*)

## For repairs of all sorts:

- [ ] Duct tape and/or packing tape
- [ ] Extension cords, power strips, adapters
- [ ] String
- [ ] Batteries
- [ ] Pocket knife
- [ ] Light bulbs
- [ ] Safety pins
- [ ] Tool set

## For laundry:

- [ ] A huge container of laundry detergent
- [ ] Fabric softener
- [ ] Stain lifter
- [ ] Rolls of quarters (well, you might not want to pack these in your luggage, but you should get a whole bunch of them the first time you go to the bank at school)

## Other things you wouldn't think about:

- [ ] Wrapping paper and ribbon
- [ ] Camera and film
- [ ] Tissues
- [ ] Envelopes
- [ ] Stamps
- [ ] Stationery
- [ ] Trash bags

Remember that your dorm room will also function as your own little kitchen. Here's a list of things you might want for your culinary enjoyment:

- ☐ Microwave (if allowed)
- ☐ Small refrigerator
- ☐ Unbreakable plates, bowls & cups
- ☐ Plastic containers
- ☐ Bottle opener
- ☐ Dishwashing liquid
- ☐ Paper towels
- ☐ Hot plate (if allowed)
- ☐ Portable coffee mug (make sure it has a lid)
- ☐ Utensils
- ☐ Corkscrew
- ☐ Sponge
- ☐ One of those small, portable vacuums

When you're packing for your dorm room, remember that you will be sharing your room with a roommate. Contact her and find out what kinds of furniture or appliances she may bring so you two don't end up bringing the same thing. We'll talk more about this in the chapter on dorm decoration, but meanwhile, keep this list in mind:

- ☐ Alarm clock
- ☐ Dry-erase board & markers
- ☐ Floor lamp
- ☐ Bedding (two pillows, two sets of extra-long bed sheets, mattress pad, comforter)
- ☐ Boombox or stereo
- ☐ Bulletin board
- ☐ Desk lamp
- ☐ Wastebasket
- ☐ Wall hangings (posters, tapestries, magazine clippings)
- ☐ Sleeping bag
- ☐ Deck of cards
- ☐ Photographs to decorate your room

chapter three
# your new home: turning a shoebox into a palace

**y**ou're standing in the hallway next to all of your boxes piled two feet over your head, and you look inside your new room and wonder, "How am I going to fit all of *this* into *that*?" It looks about as easy as fitting into a pair of jeans from fifth grade. Well, it can be done. With luck, you didn't pack more than the necessities in the first place (see the packing list in the previous chapter), but if you did you can always send the surplus home (home = storage). Not only do you have to worry about fitting everything in there, but also about turning it into your ideal bedroom, dining room, lounge, and kitchen all at the same time. You've got to transform this little shoebox into your very own palace.

Thankfully, in most colleges, the essential pieces of furniture will already be provided for you: bed, desk, chair, closet, and dresser. In addition to the essentials and appliances I listed in the previous chapter, you may also want to consider buying the following:

☐  Futon/sofa/loveseat (if you have room)
☐  TV and VCR/DVD player
☐  Phones (buy two: one portable and one with the standard cord for when you can't find the portable one)
☐  Large calendar
☐  Mirror (full length so you can check your outfits)
☐  Small bookshelf if one isn't provided
☐  Storage boxes or bins
☐  Beanbag chair or something like it

When shopping for dorm room furniture, **think cheap.** You'll only be living in this room for a year, and you'll be better off buying your furniture cheap and then selling it at the end of the spring semester, so you won't have to worry about storage. **Keep an open mind when you shop, and don't be picky.** And DON'T buy new furniture. **Shop at thrift stores, garage sales, moving sales, or buy used furniture from your college friends.** Most college students sell their furniture at the end of the school year so keep your ears and eyes open for these sales around mid-May at schools in your hometown. Or, it may be a good idea to buy furniture at your school so in the fall you've got less stuff to bring and you know how much space you have.

**Use all your space. If you don't have room, make some. You CAN.** The best way to optimize your dorm space is by lofting your bed. However, lofts often aren't permitted at many colleges, so make sure they are before you buy or build anything. If they aren't, compromise by elevating your bed with cinderblocks, which are cheap and available at any hardware store. Use big plastic bins, or even the boxes you brought your stuff over in (if they fit), to store things underneath your bed. You can hide your new storage space by using some fabric or another sheet as a bedskirt. Pick up some extra cinderblocks and wood planks at the hardward store and construct yourself some makeshift bookshelves.

Depending on how you decide to map out your social life, you may be spending lots of time in your dorm room, or you may hardly be there at all. *If you plan on making your abode the center of social activity, make it exciting. If you tend to seek other locations for partying, don't stress so much about making your dorm appealing.* **No matter what, make it comfortable, and make it yours,** because it is *your* room.

*Sort of.* **Remember you may have a roommate with whom you will be sharing your space.** Consult her before you paint a life-size self-portrait on the ceiling or construct your own replica of the Empire State Building in the center of the room. Compromise with her, but also find some space that you can make your own.

## Go to a fabric store.

It's unbelievable what you can find there and how cheap everything is. You can buy patterned fabrics to use as wall hangings, to cover ugly sofas or futons, or to use as tablecloths, curtains, and room dividers. You can also find thick and furry fabric to cut and shape into your very own makeshift rug. If you are feeling especially crafty, sew your own pillowcases. By choosing your own designs and mixing and matching, you can give your dorm room whatever look you want. And you can do it cheaply!

**Pick a color scheme.** Choose two or three different colors that complement each other and try to coordinate the things in your room with them. Determine your color scheme by picking the most noticeable colors from one of your favorite wall hangings (your framed poster of Van Gogh's *Starry Night*, for example), or one major piece of furniture.

## Decorate according to a theme.

Choose from the following, or make up your own:

- Cartoons or comic strips
- Sky (clouds, sun)
- Neon, black light, lava lamps
- Disney
- Movies or TV shows
- Animals (wild or domestic)
- Sports
- Butterflies or other insects
- Outer space (glow-in-the-dark stars, moon, planets)
- Jungle safari
- Music (band posters, ticket stubs)
- '60s or '70s retro or disco

**Paint!** Most colleges do allow you to paint your walls, as long as you paint them back to their original color before you vacate at the end of the school year. Before you even pick up a paintbrush, check with maintenance to see if it's okay. If it is, go for it. **The wall is your canvas.** It could be as simple as painting the wall a brighter color, like yellow or orange, or if you are an artist, recreating one of your own pieces of artwork, or beginning a new mural. Remember, though, that painting your walls a dark color like red, purple or navy will make the room look smaller and darker, while lighter colors make the room look more spacious. Perhaps you can strike a balance by only painting one or two walls a dark color, if you choose to use one.

## Don't forget you also have a ceiling!

It is yet another wall to account for, even if it is over your head. USE IT. Decorate it, paint it, hang things from it. Mobiles are fun to make no matter how old you are.

As I said before, the wall is your canvas. What goes on there will be reflective of your personality. So when it comes to wall décor, be selective. Don't just tear out random magazine ads and put them up. **Posters are cool, but pictures of people you know and places you've been are even cooler. Don't buy posters at your school's bookstore** unless you want your wall to sport the same posters as everyone else. Buy a poster that doesn't just "look cool," but that also really means something to you, whether it's from your favorite movie, a copy of your favorite painting, or an Ansel Adams photograph of a mountain you've climbed. Remember, you're not just trying to cover wall space, you're also trying to show people who you are.

**Put up lots of photos.** These can be pictures of your family and friends at home, or they can be photographs of your crazy times at school that you can put up as the year progresses. You can either put them up as is, or frame them first. Be creative with your photographs. Make collages, frame your mirror or windows with them, or tape them to the front of your door to show your visitors how social you are.

## Framing can be easy.

You don't have to buy frames. That could get expensive. Just mount a photo on the center of a square or rectangle of colored cardboard or matte board (you can get it at any art or photo store), leaving a border of at least one inch on each side. These makeshift frames can be tailored to match your color scheme, or bring out a particular color in the photograph.

Don't underestimate the value of plants and flowers (even fake ones). They can really add life to a room, even if they aren't alive. If you can handle the responsibility of watering on a regular basis, buy a nice, big, potted plant and situate it in the corner of the room. Even a small one is okay, as long as you put it somewhere visible. Just don't forget to take care of it. Think of your plant as your pet. And buy something rugged enough to survive without water during your vacations. Now, if the responsibility of another life is too much for you to handle—heck, you forget to feed *yourself* sometimes—then buy a fake plant, or a vase with fake or real flowers. With real flowers, all you have to do is let them sit there until they start to smell bad (which means they are dying), then buy a new bouquet. With fake or dried ones, you can let them sit there forever.

## Put up holiday lights!

More and more college students seem to be sporting the holiday look year-round, not just because lights are inexpensive, but also because stringing them around your room can do wonders for the ambiance. You can even find ones with cool shapes like fruits or stars. Depending on the colors you use and how many you put up, you can create an atmosphere that's romantic, or an environment fit for partying. And they also make great night-lights.

**Not only can you use your wall as a canvas, but also as a sketchbook or a notebook.**

Doodle on it, scribble reminders on it, jot down funny things your friends said that day, or recount unforgettable party moments. *Adorn your wall with your favorite quotations.* Write them on the wall yourself, print them out on your computer, or paste them directly onto your wall using adhesive lettering (which can be found at any art store). Remember, though, that you will have to return the walls back to their original state at the end of the year. So be prepared for that added hassle of putting a couple of coats of paint on the walls amid the packing stress.

**Do something new each year.** Every year of college invites a rebirth. Just keep the more sentimental items like photos of your friends and family, and throw out all your old decorations so you can start anew. Pick a new color scheme or a new theme and go with it. It's your new canvas.

# chapter four

# friend or enemy:
# getting along with your roommate

**n**ot only does your dorm room come with a bed and a desk, but also in all likelihood with a real live person. Unfortunately, much to your chagrin, this real live person won't be as willing to serve you as your coffee table or towel rack. If you've shared a room with someone before, you know how difficult it can be to define each other's space and respect each other's privacy. And in college, it won't be like sharing a room with your little sister. You won't be able to smack your roommate upside the head when she annoys you, nor will you be able to call on Mom or Dad to solve disputes. Your roommate will be at first a stranger, and depending on how you get along, she may just be your roommate (nothing more, nothing less), or she may become your best friend or your biggest enemy.

**Resist behavior that might make your roommate uncomfortable.**

This could mean walking around naked or in your bra and panties, going to the bathroom with the door open, or barging in without knocking.

**Don't be judgmental**, and refrain from having a preconceived notion of what your roommate is going to be like. She may be completely the opposite of what you expect, or she may be just plain weird (she may act like she's from a different *planet* in your opinion), but that doesn't mean you have a right to judge her. Even if she does have a strange penchant for seaweed (for a snack, as a room decoration, or a hair accessory), she is a real person, just like you. In fact, she may think you are quite the odd duck yourself (considering you nap with your eyes open and periodically yell out the names of the seven dwarves while you're sleeping). Everyone has his or her idiosyncrasies; the world would be a boring place otherwise.

**Remember that she is just your roommate.** No one ever said you had to become best friends with her, and in fact, it's probably better if you don't. Try to get along with her, but don't force it. If finding common ground with her turns out to be an impossible task, don't cry over it. There are SO many other things to worry about in college. Why let this one thing get to you? On the other hand, **don't attach yourself to her.** The two of you may decide that you are soul mates on the second day you live together, but you don't want to be glued together at the hips. The more you and your roommate depend on each other socially, the less likely you'll be motivated to go out and meet new people.

**Respect her space and belongings and hopefully she'll do the same for you.** Just because you are sharing a room does not mean that you shouldn't be able to define your own space. And try not to borrow anything from her, unless you really have to. If you do need to borrow something, *ask first.* The less you intrude on her space, the less she will intrude on yours and the better the two of you will get along.

---

**Figure out who is squeamishly modest and who is an exhibitionist—it will make your life a heck of a lot easier.** *"One of my roommates was an athlete who had clearly been used to showering with her team and being naked in front of people. She would hang her towel on the back of the living room door after she showered and then walk naked into her room. Four of my seven other roommates, however, were scared to change their clothes in front of other people. So, when one of those four happened to be sitting in the living room at the time, it led to a pretty disastrous outcome."*
— Lindsay Tracy, La Canada, California

## Don't engage in sexual activity on your roommate's furniture!

This means bed, futon, desk, chair, *anything*. And don't let her have sex on your stuff either. It seems obvious, but believe it or not, it *has* to be said.

If you have a problem with her that makes it difficult for you to be comfortable in your own room, TALK TO HER ABOUT IT. After all, it is your room too. Don't complain about her behind her back, but rather bring it up to her in a calm and reasonable manner. Be honest with her without being insulting. And be prepared to compromise or make sacrifices so both of you can be happy. Try your hardest to keep altercations and fights OUTSIDE OF THE ROOM. It's neutral territory.

> **Don't let your roommate smack you around.** *"When I got into my suite on the first day, my roommate had already moved in. She said, 'Hi. I'm your roommate Julia. I hope you don't mind, but I took the top bunk, the top three drawers, the desk in the other room, and the walk-in closet.' Stunned, I said, 'Umm ... okay. Sure ... I don't mind.' Yeah, right, I didn't mind! But it turned out that the top bunk was the most difficult for her because she came home stumbling drunk every night, the top three drawers actually turned out to have less space then my bottom two, and her desk, although in the more spacious room, was in the room with early hours and no sounds allowed, and her walk-in closet had no light in it, so she couldn't find her clothes anyway. Needless to say, I didn't feel too bad for her."*
> – Lindsay Tracy, La Canada, California

This one time, at math camp ... *"When I was a freshman, every night at midnight my strange roommate's even stranger friend, Jack, would come over to our common room. She would meet him at the doorway, they would turn and walk to her refrigerator (matching steps), open it together, reach in together and each would take a can of apple juice. They would close the refrigerator together, turn to face each other, and hold their cans of juice up at eye level for two seconds before taking a big breath, scream "JUUUUUUUUUIIIIIIIIIIIIIIIIIIIIIIICE!!!" and take three gulps. They would then turn as one back to the refrigerator, open the door together, stick their cans of juice back in, and walk back to the door, matching steps again. If Jack wanted to stay and talk to Lisa he had to wait outside in the hallway for 60 seconds before he could come back in. I kid you not. Apparently this disturbingly odd ritual originated from a math camp they both participated in during the summer before senior year. They gave me the explanation multiple times as I often asked them what the heck they were doing (for which I received strike-you-dead-right-here glares), but somehow I tuned it out each time, so I never really learned what the whole thing was all about."*

– Hilary McQuaide, San Francisco, California

**Make rules. Even if it seems silly to do so, they are necessary.** Even if your roommate and you seem to be getting along swimmingly, there's no telling what button you might push later on that could really set her off. Anticipate problems, and make rules to prevent them. Decide on who showers first in the morning and how often you can have overnight guests. And if a problem arises that you didn't anticipate, make a rule to prevent it from happening later.

**Don't give in to DRAMA. If getting along with your roommate is your biggest problem in life, you're LUCKY.** It's easy to make a big deal out of issues with your roommate, but if you look at the big picture, things probably aren't as bad as they seem. Don't let the little things get to you. If you don't get along with her, spend less time in your room. Study in the library. You should get out more anyway. There are so many other people to meet and places to be in college that it really isn't worth it to let one person ruin your experience, even if you do live with her. And anyway, you only really need to go to your dorm room to sleep.

**Don't go after the same guy.** This could get ugly. If she doesn't seem to agree with this rule, be the more mature person and let her have him. Guys in college usually end up being more of a pain in the neck anyway. They aren't worth a catfight with your roommate.

**If things are REALLY BAD, or even the slightest little bit life-threatening, then move out.** It is a possible solution. If you complain enough (and get your parents involved), your college dean will make the arrangements for you. But use this only as a last resort.

---

**Roommate? Or Mom away from home?** *"My roommate, an uber-nice Midwesterner (for convenience's sake, the UNM), didn't initially appear to be a problem, as I myself am a fairly nice Midwesterner. However, relations between the person in question and the rest of my suite rapidly diminished after she started treating us like her preadolescent daughters. I still don't understand this phenomenon—she did little annoying things like calling us all 'kiddo' or 'sweetie,' which was irritating but tolerable. This quickly escalated into manic parental overprotectiveness—she wouldn't let me go outside to have a cigarette by myself after dark, even if I was just going to sit on the bench outside the dorm. She would also stay up past her usual (early) bedtime on weekends to wait until all of us were back in the suite ... and it was often a long, painful wait. Once, early in the year, when one of my roommates was out past three, the UNM threatened to go out, search all of campus, find the missing suitemate, drag her back, and put her to bed. Is this normal? I think not."*

– Sarah Chihaya, Cleveland, Ohio

Be open-minded and don't jump to conclusions, but trust your instincts. If you see anything that makes you uncomfortable or afraid, tell a professor, RA, or dean immediately. *"I have a friend who goes to college in Indiana. During her sophomore year, she was rooming with a girl she thought was a friend. This girl—let's call her 'Muffy'—got odder and odder as the first semester wore on. A few times, my friend returned to her room to find Muffy and her friend, Paula, engaged in 'dark blood rituals.' My friend discovered that Muffy slept with a knife underneath her pillow. One day, Muffy accused my friend of trying to murder her by means of pillow suffocation, and Paula backed Muffy up. My friend was immediately put into a small room with three people questioning her, and was only allowed to have one friendly person in the room with her (a professor) and that person was not allowed to speak to defend her. Even though Muffy and Paula took off soon after and no one at the college really believed that my friend would try to kill anyone, the dean wouldn't admit to making a mistake, so my friend was put on disciplinary probation, meaning that even though at the time she was a double major with a minor and getting good grades in all her classes, she would not be allowed to graduate with honors, and also meaning that she is not allowed to go abroad. If it weren't for the fact that this girl has been my best friend since third grade, I would have a hard time believing this. Even so, I'm fairly sure it's not a common problem, and nothing to worry about; however, should your roommate start sleeping with a knife under her pillow and practicing blood magic, perhaps it would be a good idea to keep an eye on her."*

– Becca Crawford, Oberlin, Ohio

# chapter five

# why you are here: choosing and surviving classes

**n**ow that you've settled into your new home and (hopefully) started to form somewhat of a relationship with your roommate, you've got to think about class. That *is* why you're here, remember? With everything else going on in college, somehow classes seem to just kind of *get in the way*. You've got new people to meet, parties to go to, and guys to pursue ... who wants to waste time on *classes*? Well, no one *wants* to, but unfortunately, if you don't, you fail, then you're out, which means bye bye to all the fun as well. Classes are going to be quite different from the classes you took in high school. You're going to spend less time staring at a blackboard and more time studying and writing papers. It will take a while to get used to college life on top of your academics (or vice versa), but it is possible. It all begins with choosing the right classes.

## choosing classes

Don't rely on the course descriptions, rely on other students. Those one-paragraph descriptions don't mean a thing. **Talk to other students who have taken the class you're considering before**, or just ask upperclassmen what courses they recommend. The course descriptions may be deceiving, and only the students know the real story.

**The professor makes the course.** Ask around about good professors. The course content doesn't matter as much as how engaging the professor is. Or, talk to the professor yourself. The best ones are often willing to talk to anyone who's interested in what they are doing. The material could be exactly what you're looking for, but the professor may have a habit of droning on in monotone until the entire lecture hall has been lulled to sleep.

## Dabble.

This is the perfect time to take classes in the most random subject areas. You'll be surprised at all the interesting courses to choose from, and remember, these are the only four years in which you will really have the chance to learn something new in this kind of environment. If you are more of a math and science person, take a Shakespeare class. If you like to read and write poetry, try taking a chemistry course. There will be classes covering topics that you didn't even know existed. Take them.

**Lecture vs. seminar.** Try to even out your schedule between lectures and seminars. Here's a summary of the major differences between the two:

| Lecture | Seminar |
|---|---|
| Size: About forty to a few hundred students | About six to twenty students (usually ten) |
| Often supplemented by a small discussion section that meets for an extra hour per week | In discussion format, in which the students engage in discussion of the material, with the professor or teaching assistant as mediator |
| Usually for survey courses or introductory courses, those meant to cover a wide range of material without going into too much depth (this is mostly true for courses in the humanities, and not the sciences) | Usually for higher level courses, those covering less material in greater depth |

| Lecture | Seminar |
| --- | --- |
| You'll need to discipline yourself to do the reading on your own—you may end up cramming when the exam approaches | You have no choice but to keep up with most of the reading if you want to appear knowledgeable in class discussion |
| Less interaction with the professor and more interaction with the teaching assistant | More interaction with the professor since the class is so much smaller |
| You don't miss much if you miss a class; usually you can get notes from someone else or learn from the reading (and sometimes the professors even post their lecture notes online) | You may miss a lot if you miss a class because your participation is important to your grade |
| You take notes in class, and then pick and choose what to read from the assigned reading depending on what the professor seems to stress | You learn the material by discussing whatever you and your classmates are interested in examining further |
| You will most likely be evaluated with a final exam covering the most pertinent information | You will most likely be evaluated with a final paper in which you develop your own argument based on your interests |

**Don't worry too much about your major until sophomore year.** Unless you've already decided to take the premed or engineering route, you don't really have to worry about taking classes in a prospective major during your first year of college. In fact, don't even think about your major yet. No matter what you think you want to major in when you get there, you'll probably change your mind later. Come sophomore year, start considering a major and taking a few classes in that major. But don't make any solid decisions yet. Keep an open mind. **Most colleges don't require you to declare your major until the end of your sophomore year.** Take full advantage of all the time you have to decide.

**Don't forget about distribution requirements.** If you can, try to get those out of the way as soon as possible. And anyway, these requirements encourage you to take courses in all disciplines, which you *should* be doing. If you get the distribution requirements out of the way in your first two years of school, you can use that time to really figure out what it is you are interested in, what you want to major and minor in. Then you can spend the last two years focusing on your true interests and taking some fun electives on the side, without having to worry about requirements.

## "Major" Dialogue

Can't figure out what to major in? Try engaging in some intellectual conversation with your peers. Your answers might help you determine your calling.

**Philosophy Major:** Is the glass half empty or half full?

**Environmental Studies Major:** Well, is the glass recyclable?

**Design Major:** What's the shape and style of the glass?

**Physics Major:** If we calculate the forces acting upon the glass, factoring in gravitational pull ...

**Undecided Major:** I think the glass is full ... no, no, it's empty ... actually, it's *semi-full* ...

**When choosing classes, pay attention to the fine print.** *This means exam dates, class times, and whether you have a final exam or a final paper instead.* As strange as it sounds, you can keep all these factors in mind when deciding on your class schedule. If you fare better on papers than you do on exams, then take classes that only have papers. If you're not so much a morning person, only take classes in the afternoon. If you need more than just one day to study for a final exam, then schedule your classes so that your final exams are spread out. These factors don't necessarily have to be huge ones, but keep them in mind. One of the best things about college is that you actually have these kinds of options.

Attend the class first before you decide, if that's possible. Some colleges have a "shopping period" that might last a week or two, in which you can "shop" different classes first, before you figure out your final class schedule. If your school allows for this (rather than having you register for classes before you even get there), take advantage of it. Shop as many classes as you can in order to get a feel for what they are like. This way you can find out for yourself what the professor's like and how heavy the workload is. If you don't have the freedom to shop before registering, register for one or two more classes than necessary, and drop the ones you end up disliking.

**If you really, really want to get into a popular class that has limited enrollment, talk your way into it.**

Believe it or not, I'd say about 75 percent of the time, it will work. Talk to the professor yourself, showing him or her your enthusiasm for the course. Tell him or her that you've read their work and are planning on writing your senior thesis on a related topic. Assert that you are considering majoring in the department and you believe this class will help you decide. Even if you really aren't considering this, you never know what will happen, and more importantly, neither does the professor. If you're persistent enough, you'll get what you want. And smile a lot, too. It can only help your chances.

Start off with a light course load. You've got so many adjustments to make your first semester, the least you can do for yourself is keep classes down to a minimal stress level. And remember, you're supposed to be making friends at this point. If you want to stay in the loop, you don't want to lock yourself in the library all day to get all the studying done for six classes. Start easy. Then, once you get used to college classes, you can slowly challenge yourself. Sophomore and junior year, take the harder classes. You've probably found a solid circle of friends by then who won't turn their backs on you when you need to hit the books. But plan your schedule so that **in your senior year, you can lighten the load again a little bit.** By then, you may be writing an honor's thesis, and you'll also be applying to jobs and thinking about life after college. Plus, it will be your last year with all your friends, and you'll want to spend as much time with them as possible.

## The debate on "GUT" courses. To take them, or not to take them?

"Gut" or "bird" courses are referred to as such because they're easy, and you just fly right through them. On the one hand, taking such pushover courses allows you to concentrate on the other more important classes in your schedule and eke out a little more of a social life. On the other hand, you are paying all this money for an education, so why waste time on pointless classes? **The verdict:** Taking an easy class once in a while can't hurt, as long as you are at least moderately interested in the material. Don't take a class in a subject you despise just because it's famed to be an easy course. In fact, it may not be so easy for you in particular because of your lack of interest in the subject matter. And sometimes professors find out about the fame of their gut courses and suddenly decide to make the classes much more difficult.

# surviving classes

Once you've chosen your classes, the next thing to do is to figure out how to *survive* them. This involves managing your time, adopting good study habits, and learning how to write papers effectively. And if you can't do any of these things (which may be the case your first semester), earning decent grades will involve cramming and pulling all-nighters. However, decent grades or not, you will undoubtedly benefit from doing your best to get through your classes.

Start off on the right foot by knowing your due dates, deadlines, exam dates. Mark on your calendar when every paper is due and when every test is scheduled. Label every oral presentation, and every problem set due date. Once you've done that, hang up the calendar right above your desk, or right by your mirror, or right next to your bed. Anywhere you won't be able to avoid looking at it. This way you will at least know ahead of time when things are due, and you can start planning early. Hopefully the sight of the huge red marks on days fast approaching will scare you into getting your act together for the next assignment or exam.

Look at your calendar at the beginning of each week, and start to set your own mini-deadlines. The more time you spend in school and managing classes, you'll start to get to know yourself and how much time you need for writing papers and for studying for exams. You might have a good sense of that already. If you know that you'll need a good eight days to write a decent eight-page literary analysis on Shakespeare's *The Tempest*, then get to work on it eight days before it's due, perhaps with the goal of writing one page a day. If you've got an entire semester to write a 20-page research paper on the Cold War, allot a certain number of weeks for research, a certain number for drafting, and perhaps the last week for editing and revision.

## The Top 5 Ways 'A-' Students End Up With a 'C+'

1. Missing too many classes (whether it's because of extracurriculars or hangovers).
2. Not talking enough in class (even if you're shy, just say SOMETHING, or at least nod as though interested).
3. Getting on the professor's bad side (like writing a paper that blatantly disagrees with his ideas).
4. Asking for too many paper extensions (if you make a habit of it, your prof will think you don't care).
5. Waiting till the last minute for your research and finding all the books gone (even if you aren't planning on writing your paper until the night before, at LEAST get the books in advance!).

## Pulling an all-nighter?

Make sure you are well-equipped. You'll need:

- cold water (to drink and to splash on your face when you need a pick-me-up)
- an open window (to keep you refreshed and awake)
- peanut M&Ms (carbs for a quick energy boost, and you *can't* go wrong with chocolate)
- trail mix
- alarm clock or watch
- sweatpants
- music (not too loud, just barely audible to keep you awake)
- every reference book and library book you could possibly need

**Give yourself more time than you think you need.** You never know what might come up, so it's better to get a head start on things. You may be halfway done with a paper and suddenly want to change your topic. You may want to start early so you can leave some time to meet with your professor or teaching assistant and get some feedback on where you're headed with your paper.

**Don't be afraid to ask for help.** Your professors and teaching assistants are there for a reason. Ask them for help if you have trouble applying a certain formula, or don't know where to go from your thesis, or aren't sure how to study for the midterm. **Don't be scared by your professors, as intimidating as they might be. They were once freshmen too.** And you can also ask your classmates, and even tutors that are often available for people who might need a little bit of guidance. Ask the cute boy who sits in front of you for some assistance. Hmm, maybe the two of you can work together on the next problem set ...

It might work for some people ... *"I remember thinking during freshman year that all of the libraries on campus were rather dark and dreary places to be studying or writing papers. Particularly the main library, which was housed in a building that looked like a Gothic cathedral, suffered from a severe lack of windows and indoor lighting, and maintained a room temperature of about 85 degrees at any given point in the year. The chairs were hard, and the couches were uncomfortable. Doing work in the library clearly wasn't going to work. Finally, I decided to set up my laptop at the foot of my bed, bottom bunk and all, and set up the printer underneath my bed. It was great. I didn't even have to change out of my pajamas to study at any hour of the day or night, and I never felt stupid falling asleep, as I would have in the library. The habit stuck through all four years of college, and I've probably taken more catnaps in the midst of assignments than anyone else, but hey, I got the work done!"*

– Alice Ko, Diamond Bar, California

**Pace yourself so you don't have to cram later.** Cramming sucks. And the thing is, it's easy to avoid if you do the reading you're supposed to do for each week. Honestly, if, starting at the beginning of the semester, you spend just two hours in the library studying every day, you will have less cramming to do come final exam time. Every one of your classes will load you with hundreds of thousands of pages of reading to do. **You don't want to try to do all that reading the night before the exam.**

## Study in different places.

At a café. In the bookstore. In a coffee shop. On a bench outside. On the grass. At the local diner. In the dining hall. In an empty classroom. On the bleachers at the gym. In a courtyard. On a hammock. On a swing. On a rooftop.

Having trouble sounding intellectual in your discussion section? Here are a few buzzwords you can use to blow away your classmates and professor:

**declension** (n): deviation or declining from a standard; sinking into a lower or inferior condition

EXAMPLE: I am very disappointed in the quick declension of this sweater I just bought; it has already begun to unravel!

**dialectic** (adj): of, pertaining to, or of the nature of logical disputation; argumentative, logical

EXAMPLE: When what began as lighthearted dinner conversation with Mom and Dad turned into dialectic discussion, I regretted having invited my boyfriend over that night.

**dichotomy** (n): division of a whole into two parts

EXAMPLE: There seems to be a dichotomy within the group: some of us want to go to the movies, and some of us want to get a bite to eat. Why don't we just do both?

**exegesis** (n): explanation, or exposition of a sentence, word, or passage

EXAMPLE: Her detailed exegesis of the Shakespeare excerpt helped me to understand it much better than CliffsNotes ever could.

**hermeneutic** (adj): belonging to or concerned with interpretation

EXAMPLE: The meaning of the lyrics is purely hermeneutic: it could be about love to one person, or friendship to another. It just depends on how you decide to look at it.

**juxtaposition** (n): the action of placing two or more things close together or side by side

EXAMPLE: The juxtaposition of these shoes and this shirt just isn't working for me. They don't match at all!

**quotidian** (adj): of or pertaining to everyday; ordinary, commonplace, trivial

EXAMPLE: Let's not go out for pizza this time around; it seems rather quotidian for this special occasion. How about sushi?

**Study in an environment that's comfortable, but not too comfortable.** This may take a while to figure out, but during your first semester at college, try studying in different environments in order to figure out which one allows you to get work done more effectively. Know yourself and how much or how little noise you prefer in your work environment. And, if at all possible, avoid studying in your room. Your room is where you sleep, where you hang out, where there are lots of distractions.

**Take study breaks!** Reward and motivate yourself in the midst of studying by taking a break once in a while. If you're in the middle of what you expect to be a five-hour stretch of psychology textbook reading, allow yourself to take a break every time you finish a chapter. But don't let your study break last any longer than necessary. A half-hour is quite enough time. Or try taking a ten minute study break every hour. If you're pulling an all-nighter, perhaps an hour is sufficient, but nothing more.

## A quick study break can do wonders for your progress.

Make yourself a snack. Climb a tree. Lift weights. Play solitaire. Visit a friend upstairs, with milk and cookies in hand. Pluck your eyebrows. Get a slice of pizza. Look through your photo album. Go for a run. Check your mailbox. Write poetry. Paint your toenails. Talk on Instant Messenger (but not for too long— don't get hooked!). Do a self-portrait. Hit the local music store and buy a new CD. Call a friend from home. Give yourself a makeover. Take a shower. Write a letter. Dance to your favorite Madonna song. Get some ice cream. Play a video game. Shop online. Make a photo collage. Doodle. Burn a CD of your favorite songs. Fill out one of those e-mail questionnaires. Make jewelry. Go rollerblading. Think of things to invent so you can be rich. Google search your name and your friends' names. Daydream …

**Learn the art of skimming.** Every professor always assigns about three times as much reading as a normal human being is actually capable of doing. Don't try to read everything. Skim. **This means reading the introduction, the first and last sentences of every paragraph, and the conclusion.** This gives you a general idea of the material, and is most effective in classes that evaluate you with exams rather than papers.

## Don't rely so much on study groups.

Study groups can be very helpful. They can make studying much more fun and less stressful, but they can also be a waste of time. Study with other people only after you've done a ton of studying on your own first. Don't think of the study group as your only source of preparation for an exam. You'll be expecting too much.

## Got some memorizing to do? Look in the mirror.

If you're like me, you use your mirror at least two or three times a day to check your outfit, your hair, or your make up. Or even to do a little eyebrow plucking when you spot some stray hairs. If you've got to memorize some formulas or definitions, use a dry erase marker and write everything on the mirror in your dorm room. That way, every time you look at yourself, you won't even realize that you're doing some studying at the same time.

**Become even better at the art of selective reading.** This approach works better for classes that evaluate more based on your participation in class discussion and also on analytical papers. When you read selectively, you don't just skim, nor do you read everything. Rather, you **read a few well-chosen texts in depth.** This way, you may not know all the material, but you do know a few important things in very good detail. **If you are able to discuss these things in class, the professor will assume that you have done all the necessary reading.** And, when it comes to writing a paper, you can focus your topic only on the texts that you have actually read. In fact, you might even wait until you receive the next paper assignment to determine which texts are important, or read the texts

## Use your first paper assignment as a gauge.

Every professor grades differently and every professor stresses a different aspect of the analytical essay, whether it is the strength of the argument, the clarity of writing, the writing style, or the strength of the evidence. Once you've been graded on your first paper, you'll get a sense of what the professor is looking for. If you are disappointed with your grade, or any other grade for that matter, don't whine about it, but don't be afraid to ask your professor why you received it.

that the professor seems to emphasize the most. Or, ask people who took the class last year what was important.

Paper-writing in college is much different than it was in high school. You aren't just writing the standard five-paragraph essay anymore. I wish I could give you the exact formula for writing a perfect paper. **But the fact is, it all depends on what the professor is looking for.** Do your best to come up with an original argument that is interesting enough to you that you feel confident writing a paper on it. Come up with a thesis and run it by your professor well before the paper is due. Along with your thesis, try to give him or her a general idea of how you plan to organize your essay and what evidence you will use to back up your argument. If your professor likes where you're headed, then it's likely that ultimately he or she will be satisfied with your paper.

## It's all in the title.

The title of an essay can make or break your grade. Well, not really, but almost all of your professors will want you to have a title, and it's important that the title is indicative of the quality of your paper. Thankfully, there's actually a formula for this, and you can even come up with a title long before you've written the paper itself! To create a paper title, use the **[X]: [Y] in [Z] model**. In this model:

X **is a quote or phrase** from the work or from some other literary resource, at least slightly relevant to your topic

Y **is the subject matter** you're writing about

Z **is the name of the author or text** you're writing about.

Ex.: **"The Cupboard Under the Stairs": Child Abuse and Neglect in Rowling's** *Harry Potter*

# money talk: personal finance

**m**oney doesn't grow on trees, they say, and when you're in college, you'll wish it did, or at least that you could barter the tacky gold charm bracelet your grandmother gave you for a meal or two instead of having to hand over some green. For some reason, college students are always low on cash. Perhaps it's because most of us would rather party hard than get a job; or maybe it's because we don't know how to manage our money (cash seems to disappear into thin air come the weekend); or, hmm ... maybe it's because tuition these days seems to cost more than the monetary value of an island in the Pacific. Whatever the reason, you're going to have to earn some money in college, whether it's just for your own spending money, or to help pay for tuition. And once you have some earnings, you've got to learn to save it and spend it wisely.

# get a job

"Is she nuts?" you think to yourself. How on earth am I supposed to find time to work on top of classes, studying, friends, partying, extracurriculars, working out, dating, and not to mention eating and sleeping?? Believe it or not, it's possible. It depends on how much of a priority money is to you, but chances are, it's a *major* priority, so it might be worth dropping an extracurricular activity or two. Fortunately, college campuses are filled with jobs that you'll be able to fit into your schedule one way or another.

**Work on campus.** Once you've settled in, check out the student employment office for on-campus job listings. **On-campus jobs tend to**

allow more flexibility for your busy schedule. Also, these jobs often pay much better than similar jobs off campus. Your employers are more understanding of the fact that you are a college student and have five hundred other things to make time for. You will probably be able to make your own hours, and heck, if you need to miss work so you'll have a few more hours to finish up a term paper, you probably can, as long as you call in. Your boss will most likely recognize that you are a student before everything else, so he or she will let you off the hook for academic reasons.

On the other hand, working off-campus might be better for you if you want to get away. Some students prefer off-campus jobs because it's a way of escaping the college grounds for a little while. It's a great way to meet people from the area who don't attend your college, and to become familiar with the world outside your campus. The downside is that your employer may not have mercy on you if you've got three papers to write on a weekend that he has you working double shifts, *both* days. To him, you're an employee first, and a student second.

## No matter where you work, always bring some studying.

You never know when you'll have some free time to do some reading for one of your classes, and believe me, you'll want to use it. Just be discreet about cracking open a textbook in the office. You don't want to look like a slacker.

When you're on the job search, consider how many hours you want to work, and when. It's important to have a set idea of how many hours you want to work per week (most college students work an average of five to ten hours per week at an on-campus job). Then decide whether you want to work during the day, or on evenings and weekends. Make sure your hours fit around your class schedule. Most offices are only open Monday through Friday, nine to five. If with classes and other activities you find it hard to put in hours during the day, there are on-campus jobs available in which you can work evenings and weekends, for example at a library, a computer lab, or a cafeteria. Or, if you choose to work off-campus, you can baby-sit, wait tables, or work in retail.

**Accept that you might not be working the most fun or glamorous job in the world. In fact, you might just be doing the grunt work.** Particularly if you are working on campus in an office, you probably won't be having very much fun. Making copies, filing, sorting mail, and answering phones may not be the most exciting tasks in the world, but just take comfort in the fact that those measly chores are putting money in your pocket. Some jobs, like those at the library, pay you by the hour to sit at a desk and study while you wait for the phone to ring or for someone to check out a book.

**Try to look for a job related to your career path.** Don't worry so much about this during your first couple years at college, but it's something to think about as graduation (and your entrance into the *real* job market) approaches. Even if a job in the field you are interested in might pay *much* less than, say, waiting tables, it might be worth the sacrifice. Resume-building can never start too early.

---

*"I came to college freshman year with more than $2,000 in the bank. By the end of first semester, I had about $300. I didn't realize just how expensive EVERYTHING is at college. 'Textbooks' were the same size as first-grade readers and cost $35, never mind the ones that I couldn't even fit into my backpack and had to pay for in three installments. The other things that sucked up my money were pizza and beer, and, of course, new clothes (we won't say why my old ones didn't fit me anymore, that's another topic). So, I got a job. It's easy to get your paycheck and spend it immediately, so I opted for direct deposit into my savings account. That way, the money didn't go straight to my debit card and I wasn't totally broke by the end of my first year at school."*

— Arija Weddle, Fairfield, Connecticut

## Cheap Ways to Have Fun in College

**For the young at heart:**
*Game Night.* Board games, that is. The last board game you played may have been Candyland when you were five or so, but this doesn't mean that you won't have fun playing board games in college. Pick a game that is interactive and energized, like Taboo, Pictionary, or Encore. Make sure you have some snacks available, and if need be, spice things up with some alcohol (preferably *cheap* beer—we're trying to stick to a budget, here).

**For the girly-girl:**
*Spa Night.* Invite the girls over and tell them to bring their nail polish, face masks, and makeup. Spend the night watching cheesy '80s movies and pampering yourselves.

**For the movie buff:**
*Movie Night.* Pick a theme and then invite your friends to dress up according to the theme and come watch the movie of choice. For example, have an island adventure theme, watch movies set on an island or beach, dress up in sarongs and bikinis, drink piña coladas. Or, watch *Chocolat* and *Like Water for Chocolate*, and drink mudslides to wash down some Hershey's chocolate.

**For the philosopher:**
*Stogie Smoking.* Find a rooftop on any building nearby and bring some matches and a really cheap cigar. This one's great for late-night, deep conversations.

**For the athlete:**
*Miniature Golf.* Mini-golf is cheap, and you can make the most of it by grabbing the ball before the last hole eats it, and then you can go through the entire course over and over again!

**For the partier:**
*Potluck Party.* You want to throw a party, but you can't afford it. Here's a simple solution: You provide the location, and have your guests provide the food, drinks, and music. Everyone who attends has to bring something in order to get past the front door, whether it's a bag of chips, a CD with some fun dance music, some paper plates, a six pack, or a container of macaroni and cheese.

# conserve your cash

Now that you have a pocket full of dough, you've got to make sure it doesn't slip through your fingers too easily. Once you're handed a paycheck every Friday, you may be quite tempted to cash it in and get to partying, but you've *got* to be strong. The cash may have gone to a seemingly worthwhile night of revelry, but you'll wish you had it later when you get your next phone bill.

**Open up a checking account.** Say *sayonara* to your piggy bank, or to that shoebox under your bed, because it's time to keep your money where the grownups do. Deposit your money in a checking account, and make sure you get a checkbook and an ATM card. This way your money is in a safe place, and you'll be able to keep track of where it goes much more easily. It may also be a good idea to open up a savings account also. Put a small amount of every paycheck into your savings account each week. Vow not to use that money unless you're in a bind, and this way you'll have a growing reserve of money that you can fall back on in the future.

**Keep track of all your expenses.** Make a record of how much you spend in a typical week. If you find that fifty percent of it goes to pizza or take-out, you might want to evaluate your spending habits. Monitoring your own spending will help you look for ways you can save money.

Credit cards are EVIL. You should definitely have a credit card, but use it ONLY IN AN EMERGENCY. If you use a credit card more than necessary you'll start spending money you don't have, and you can accumulate a huge credit card debt without even realizing it. (Keep in mind that if you have loans covering your tuition, you're already going to be in the hole when you graduate—there's no reason to dig yourself deeper with big credit card bills.) Only use it when you absolutely need to, and when you know you'll be able to pay off the debt quickly.

## A few ways to save your moolah:

1. **Put a cap on those long distance phone calls** to your mom or your boyfriend. Besides, you're a big girl now, and you don't need to be calling Mom that often. And you're supposed to have broken up with your high school boyfriend by now, remember? Now, if you can't bear to cut down, *consider investing in a cell phone*. Most cell phone plans give you free long distance and a huge number of minutes per month for a set fee. Or, even better, chat with family and friends on the computer, or communicate via e-mail instead.

2. **Buy used textbooks rather than new ones**. Keep your eyes open around campus for flyers advertising used book sales by older students. Your college's bookstore might even sell used copies of their books as well. Used book websites are also a terrific resource. Or, better yet, *borrow books from the library instead of buying them*.

3. **If you are a coffee addict, buy your own coffee machine for your dorm room.** You may not notice, but your ritualistic morning (and afternoon, AND evening) excursions to the coffee shop on the corner will slowly deplete your cash reserve.

4. **If you smoke, quit.** You'll save money, AND your lungs.

5. **See matinee movies at the theater instead of evening showings.** Better yet, rent movies.

6. **Only eat out at restaurants or order take-out on special occasions.** You've probably already paid for the meal plan, so even if the food sucks, you might as well eat it if it will save you money. Otherwise, *cook your own food.* If you have a buffet cafeteria, take extra fruit, sandwiches and other snacks for later on at night.

7. **If you're older than twenty-one, limit your purchases of alcoholic beverages.** Those purchases add up, even if you do just buy cheap beer. Instead of buying your own alcohol, go to fraternity or house parties that supply beverages for free. Try not to go to bars to have fun. Drinks at bars can get expensive. If you must choose a bar as a location to meet up with friends, become a drink special aficionado. Almost all bars have drink specials on certain nights or at certain times of day or night.

8. **Walk, bike, or rollerblade whenever possible.** You'll save on gas or public transportation, and hey, you may also shed a few pounds with all that additional exercise.

# chapter seven

# personal well-being: taking care of yourself

p icture this: you, just having rolled out of bed for your 8:30 a.m. class, hair in a knotted ponytail, dark circles under your glassy eyes, fumbling across campus in jeans that *used* to fit but now feel kind of tight due to the spare two inches around your waist that also seem to be slowing your pace to class. You could care less. Whatever. Lately you've been kicking butt in school thanks to your routine of all-nighters every weeknight, and they give you free soda at the local pizza place since you go there so often for your late-night snacks. Life is *good*, you think to yourself. You're surprised you somehow managed to mentally string these three words together while in your near-comatose state, as you jam your favorite powdered doughnut down your throat and wash it down with some black coffee. It ain't a pretty sight.

It's a sight that's not so rare for the typical college girl. You get so wrapped up in this juggling act you forget to show love to the person who needs it the most. The juggler: yourself. Without her, everything falls to the floor. Remember: **With all the changes that will be going on in your life in the next four years, the one thing that will always remain constant is yourself.** So, *take care of yourself*—physically, mentally, and emotionally. College life is hard enough already. Don't make it harder by depriving yourself of sleep, exercise, and a healthy diet. It's no fun to study for final exams with a 102-degree fever or strep throat slowing you down and making you miserable.

First things first: **the freshman fifteen.** According to this widely-held belief, every freshman in college gains fifteen pounds by the time the year comes to a close. But this is a myth. The truth is that college is a time of fluctuation in weight and overall health for many people, but the freshman fifteen is not universal. The fact is, in your first year of college you will be going through many changes, including changes in the way you eat and how you take care of your body. Some people do gain a few pounds, others lose a few. And some people experience no major physical changes at all. Don't live in fear of the freshman fifteen because, for all you know, it may not apply to you. What's important is that you take care of your body so you can love the person you are no matter how you look or how much you weigh.

# exercise!

If you are an athletic person, then exercise may already be part of your routine. However, if not, taking time out of your daily schedule to work out might not be so easy. All I can say is, *too bad*. Physical fitness may not have been a priority in high school, but now that you're on your own you've got to learn to take control of your body. If you don't, the freshman fifteen just might rear it's ugly head, and once it's latched on to you, there's no telling how long it will take to get it off your back (or your tummy, rather). **Exercise is your secret weapon, and the beauty of it is, the more you exercise, the less you have to worry about how much you eat.** If you followed my advice from chapter one, you already started a workout plan before you even got to school. Remember, you've only got so much time before school starts to get used to working out every day. Once you get to school, you'll be busy and it will be easy to make excuses not to exercise. If you make working out part of your routine beforehand, not only will you be in shape to leave room for a little weight gain, but you will also be more likely to continue with your workout plan once the school year begins.

## Workouts don't always have to be planned.

Exercise if you need a study break or if you are feeling stressed out. Head to the gym or go for a run if you've got an hour to kill between classes or if other plans get cancelled.

## You don't have to go to the gym to work out.

I used to be afraid of the gym. I always feared that I would break a weight machine or fall on my face while running on the treadmill. If you have similar fears, don't go to the gym to work out. You don't have to. Jog. Power walk. Rollerblade. Bike. Swim laps. Kickbox. Practice yoga. Just get your body moving and have fun with it!

**All you need is thirty minutes a day.** A lot of people are hesitant to work out because they think that they have to sacrifice a huge chunk of time in their day to do it. If you work out for just thirty minutes every day, you're getting the workout you need. Obviously, the longer you exercise the better, but thirty minutes minimum is sufficient for a good cardiovascular workout. If you have the time, try to set aside an hour for your daily workout. And alternate between cardiovascular workouts and weight lifting. If you work out at the gym, use a stair-climber for thirty minutes, then tackle the free weights for another thirty minutes. **Vary your workout so you don't get bored.**

## There are other ways to fool yourself into getting a little workout in at random points in the day.

Schedule your classes across campus so you have to power walk or sprint from class to class. Always take the stairs. Leave ten minutes early for class and take the long way. Walk twice as fast to class. Go exploring a part of campus you don't know very well. Shake your leg in class.

**Make exercise a part of your daily routine.** Discipline yourself to work out every day. It may be difficult at first, but once you've worked out every day for a few weeks or a month, it will become a habit. In fact, you'll feel how your body changes whenever you miss a workout. **Try to**

work out at the same time every day. If you schedule a specific time for exercise, you will be far more likely to do it. Make it a necessity—a fixed part of your schedule just as important as going to class. Also, work out early in the day. It's more effective and better for you than a caffeine jolt. The earlier in the day you work out, the better you feel. Exercise gives you energy, energy that will fuel your body for the rest of the day. It's more effective and better for you than a caffiene jolt. Plus, if you do it first thing in the morning, it's over with and you won't have the chance to make an excuse for skipping the workout later on.

### Get a workout buddy.

If you have trouble motivating yourself to work out, exercise with a friend. This way the two of you can keep each other in check. You'll be less likely to skip a workout if you've got someone else to answer to.

# food (sort of)

Cafeteria food isn't exactly the most nutritional dining experience. It's possible that the grossness of cafeteria food will ensure that you DON'T overeat there. However, in many college cafeterias, it's all-you-can-eat, buffet style, so you can go for seconds and thirds and fourths. There are no limits, and sometimes it's tempting to take advantage of the lack of boundaries, even if the food is unappetizing. (Besides, you pay an insane amount of money for the meal plan already, why not milk them for all they've got?) So, watch what you eat and how much you eat. The cafeteria is often such a social place that you may find yourself spending up to two hours there hanging out with friends. In those two hours you might not even realize that you've already inhaled four cups of frozen yogurt. You are there to socialize, but since it's a cafeteria, you feel like you have to be eating the whole time. *You don't.* Have your meal, then mingle with your friends without stuffing your face.

## The later you eat, the more weight you gain.

You need to be awake and moving around to burn calories, so the food that you consume near bedtime will be more difficult to shed later. Try to keep the late-night post-drinking binges to a minimum.

Cafeterias often force you to have dinner too early, causing you to become hungry later. **Learn to manipulate the system.** Even if you show up at the dining hall right before it closes, it's highly likely you'll be up late enough to have a second dinner, or at least a late-night snack. **Take food from the dining hall.** Make yourself a sandwich, grab an apple or pear, fill a paper cup with your favorite cereal. You're paying money for this anyway, so you might as well take advantage. If you grab something to munch on later that's moderately healthy, you will be less likely to order pizza or Chinese take-out (calories, calories!!) when that craving for a second dinner arises.

## Beer is loaded with calories.

Unfortunately, you might find that beer will be your drink of choice on many occasions. Now, if you generally watch what you eat and exercise regularly, downing a few beers on the weekends won't hurt your svelte physique *too much*. But moderation, girls, moderation.

Speaking of which, resist the urge to order out for pizza every night after a bad meal at the dining hall. Dining-hall food may not be the ideal gastronomic experience, but neither is pizza or Chinese take-out. Only go out to eat or order in on special occasions, on the weekends, or when you are cramming and desparate for a study break.

A little bit of weight gain in college is not the end of the world. You can't maintain your girlish high school figure forever, and you shouldn't try to. A lot of people gain a little weight in college. If you think about it, the freshman fifteen is kind of a reassuring thing in that way because many of your peers will be putting on some pounds at the same time! Just don't get psychotic about fighting it—it's natural. Everyone goes through it.

### Eating disorders.

College is such a stressful environment, and one that also encourages you to reinvent yourself. It's difficult not to want to become the physical ideal, and fear of the freshman fifteen might put even more pressure on you. For this reason, many college women develop eating disorders such as anorexia and bulimia. They respond to the pressures and fears by not eating at all, and thereby endangering their health. If any of your friends show signs of an eating disorder, seek help. Show her that you are concerned, talk to a counselor or an eating disorder hotline for help on how to handle the situation, and if the situation seems severe, call her parents.

# sleep is good

Make sleep a priority. True, there's a lot to do in college, and now that you don't have Mom and Dad enforcing curfews, you've got eight more hours to schedule as you see fit. But this doesn't mean that using those hours for some quality sleep isn't the most effective use of time. You need to get enough sleep to think straight and survive your classes. You need to get enough sleep to function—period.

At first, you'll be so busy trying to fit everyone and everything into your schedule that sleep will be the last thing on your priority list. Then you will start to *crave* it. You'll fall asleep in class and use every free minute you have during the day for a nap.

No doubt, sometimes you will have to sacrifice sleep for other things, like studying or writing a paper. But **try to plan ahead so that you can get things done earlier and still get the sleep you need.**

**Make up for lost sleep by napping during the day, if you can.** Just try not to nap for too long (no longer than 45 minutes to an hour), otherwise you'll just feel slow and groggy the rest of the day. And make sure you set an alarm because you don't want to miss class, section, or a club meeting just because you were taking a nap. Ultimately, getting all the sleep you need at one time, at the right time (nighttime), will ensure you get the most out of it. Save the all-nighters for the weekends so you can sleep in the next day.

## Dealing with depression.

Depression is more likely to appear in women than it is in men, and it is also disturbingly common among college students. Therefore, as college women, we are especially at risk of becoming depressed, whether it is caused by relationship problems, a break-up, family problems, stress, or adjusting to the new environment. We all feel down sometimes, and we all have our good days and our bad days. But if your bad days have stretched into bad weeks or months, you may be clinically depressed. If you or someone you know is suffering from any of the following symptoms, consider seeking help:

- loss of appetite or increased appetite
- indifference, loss of interest or pleasure
- continual feelings of sadness
- withdrawal
- lack of motivation
- fatigue, lack of energy
- insomnia or oversleeping
- lack of concentration
- feelings of helplessness, hopelessness, and worthlessness
- excessive crying
- irritability
- thoughts of suicide or suicide attempts

If you think a friend is suffering from depression, encourage your friend to get help. If she chooses not to, tell a counselor who will be able to give you advice on how to handle the situation.

# stress: your biggest enemy and your most loyal companion

In college it will seem like no matter what you get done or how few commitments you make, there will always be something to stress about. Whether it's midterms, papers, sports practices, relationships, phone bills, or rehearsals, something will always be looming over your head. And as these things continue to hover, stress will rise to meet them, there to meet the challenge, but often putting you in overdrive and pushing your body into a state of anxiety. If you're under stress, not only does your mind worry constantly, but your body reacts as well. When you find yourself fighting headaches, muscle tension, insomnia, acne, or nausea, it's highly likely that you are pretty stressed out. We're lucky in that our minds and bodies tend to be synchronized; they tend to communicate with and affect each other. So, listen to your body—it's probably trying to tell you something. Sound mind, sound body.

**A healthy body yields a healthy mind.** The best way to prevent and manage stress is to exercise. Hit the gym when you feel overwhelmed. It's an incredible way of releasing stress. The more you exercise, the better you sleep, the better you concentrate, the better you look, and the better you feel. All of this will reduce your stress even more.

## Avoid excessive amounts of caffeine.

Caffeine can actually increase stress. You know you are consuming too much of it if you are having trouble sleeping or concentrating. If you are trying to stay up for an all-nighter, don't drink coffee or soda. Try drinking ice water and keeping the window open so the cool air can keep you awake.

What will stress you out the most in college is figuring out how to accomplish all the things you have to do in such a short period of time. **Don't get overwhelmed.** You might find that you are so apprehensive about the magnitude of what you have to accomplish that you just stop and give up. **Break it all down.** Yes, there's a lot to do, but you can get it done, you just have to plan it out and take it one step at a time. Make a list of all the things that are stressing you out, then make a plan that involves managing each problem separately. **You may find that what you thought were huge, unmanageable problems are really just a series of smaller, manageable tasks.**

> ## Remember there are some things you can't control, and there are some things you can't change.
>
> Learn to accept that certain things are out of your reach, so there's no point in worrying or stressing about them. You're better off keeping focused on the things you can control and the things you can change.

**Don't spread yourself thin.** Yes, college opens up a lot of doors, and there are activities you can participate in that you didn't even know existed. It's tempting to try to have your hands in everything, but the fact is, you won't be able to do it all. Be realistic about what you can fit into your schedule and about what you can expect from yourself. Besides, it's better to be an enthusiastic and dedicated member of a few clubs and activities rather than a scatterbrained, distracted member of more organizations than you can count on your fingers and toes.

**Keep your perspective.** Much of what stresses you out might not be worth stressing over. It might feel like the world is crashing down around you, but stop and think to yourself, "Will this matter a year from now?" If there are certain things that occupy your mind that you realize are not important, *let them go.* Figure out what's really worth your mental energy, and focus on that.

**Write things down.** The less you have to remember on your own the more relaxed your mind will be. Keep a datebook of all your exams, due dates, appointments, and meetings. Always keep a small pen and notebook handy wherever you go so if you remember something while you're walking down the street or eating in the

dining hall, you can jot it down before you forget. Use this notebook or keep a separate journal to write any thoughts you might have, things you wouldn't say to anyone else. The feelings that cause stress tend to fester inside you. It's best to let them out, whether it's through exercise or through expressing yourself in words.

**Stress might seem like it's something you can handle only on your own, but it doesn't have to be.**

Don't be afraid to talk to someone, whether it's a friend, a family member or a counselor. Oftentimes things get so hard to handle that you need the support of other people. Find people to talk to if you need someone to just listen, or to offer you some advice. Don't underestimate the value of other people.

Don't procrastinate. The more you put things off, the longer you worry about getting them done. Just accomplish whatever you can as soon as you have the time to do it. The sooner you do the work, the less time you will have to spend thinking about the work you have to do.

Whatever you do, confront your stress. Stress has this habit of building up, especially if it's not dealt with. Oftentimes the stress ends when the day ends, and as soon as another day begins you are stress free. But, if you find that those stress-free days are few and far between, ask for help.

**Set aside time for fun and relaxation.**

Time for yourself and with your friends in an unstressful environment is just as important as time for classes and studying. Make a point to schedule time for recreation.

# chapter eight

# getting social:
# meeting people and having fun

t hank goodness for the weekend. Friday night (or better yet, Thursday night, if you've scheduled your classes accordingly) signals the start of the weekend, which means it's time to lay those books to rest and let the games begin. It doesn't matter when you choose to free your mind of calculus and Shakespeare, just as long as you do. You need to give yourself some time in the week for the other very important half of college life: having fun and meeting new people. True, it's quite important that you make friends with your textbooks and even better friends with your professors, but I can pretty much guarantee you'll have a lot more fun with your fellow students. You no longer have the security blanket of your high school clique to help you feel socially safe come Friday night, so now you've got to find a new posse. The great thing about college is you're in this new environment, filled with people who are just as excited and bewildered as you are to be there. You've just got to meet them all, and then from there, you'll find people to hang out with on the weekends or in your downtime during the week. Well, fortunately for you, college is filled with a variety of opportunities to meet and get to know people, whether it's through organizations, events, or parties.

# meeting people

**Start off with what you're interested in.** Every college has myriad organizations that cater to everyone's different interests. And, if an organization doesn't exist for something you are interested in, you can always start one. Your school likely hosts some sort of activities fair for freshman that introduces many of these organizations to you. If not, take the initiative and go to the student activities office, or keep your eye out for postings on bulletin boards or in the college newspaper. Joining an organization is the best way to meet people who have similar interests as you. To give you an idea of what kinds of organizations you might consider joining, peruse the following list.

- **Sport or athletic activity.** This could be a varsity sport, a club sport, or an intramural sport. If you choose to join a varsity sport, be aware that it will take up lots of time. Varsity sports are for those who take the sport very seriously, whereas club or intramural sports tend to be more laid back and just for fun.
- **Student government.** This is a great way to meet people and get involved in your school.
- **School newspaper, TV, or radio station.** This is your chance to get recognized on campus, whether it's by name, face, or voice.
- **Literary magazine, science magazine, or any other publication.** If you're interested in writing, write for a publication. If none of the existing publications appeal to you, start your own magazine about whatever you want. The possibilities are endless.
- **Community service organization.** These types of organizations do everything from serving at soup kitchens to mentoring kids to building homes.
- **Choir, glee club, orchestra, band.** If music is your passion, continue with it through college. You will be among other such talents, and you'll find that music is taken much more seriously and you'll learn much more.
- **Drama or dance club, a cappella or comedy group.** If you like to perform, there are *countless* opportunities to do so. In fact, even if you never have been in a play, try out anyway if you're curious about it. I've known people who were cast in lead roles without any acting experience. Or try working behind the scenes, maybe on lights or sound, or on the stage crew.
- **Cultural group.** College is also a great place to meet people of your same culture, race, or ethnicity. A cultural group on campus is a good place to start learning about yourself.

- **Religious organization.** Most colleges have student-run religious organizations that sponsor organized activities, and provide a site in which you can meet new people with similar religious backgrounds.
- **Sorority or co-ed fraternity.** At many colleges, the entire social arena is dominated by Greek life. If your college is one of them, and you're into being well-informed of all the social haps every weekend, joining a sorority or co-ed fraternity might be just the right thing for you.

**Don't spread yourself thin.** I touched on this in the section about stress, but it's important to mention it again. As soon as you get to college you might have aspirations to join ten different organizations, and all ten of them might seem equally exciting to you. Remember, you have four whole years to try out everything you can. No need to cram everything in during your first semester, or first year, for that matter. It's better to join one or two organizations and be a dedicated member, rather than trying to attend all meetings and commitments for thirteen different clubs and publications.

Not many people (if any) are going to know anything about you besides what you bring to the table. *"This can be a time to break free from old labels, or it can be a realization that no one knows who you are or even thinks to ask. At the same time, you don't want to be that girl who overcompensates for her labels in high school because everyone can see through that and you'll be right back into that label by default. About three months into school, I was working on a theater project with a friend from class. As we swapped theater stories from high school, it dawned on us that because we had not yet been in any plays at college, our roommates and friends had no idea that theater was even a part of our lives when growing up, that it was actually our passion. No one had ever even thought to ask to see our photo albums from high school. It was devastating and scary to think that my roommates and friends at college could overlook such a large part of who I was—my past."*

– Lindsay Tracy, La Canada, California

At the same time, don't become consumed by any one organization, either. It's easy to let your membership in an organization take precedence over the rest of your life, especially if you're really into it and you hold some kind of position of authority. There's nothing wrong with dedicating yourself to anything, just as long as it doesn't become too much of a stressful (and even *not* fun) part of your life. Don't let your grades fall, your health regress, and your stress level increase because of your commitment to an organization. Remember, too, that you don't have to do anything just to please other people. It's important that you try new things, but also know it's okay not to follow through if you realize the commitment is just too much for you. You're here to experiment. If it sucks, quit. There's no point in you being miserable.

**Don't join an organization for any reason other than your personal interest in the group's activities or mission.** It may be tempting to join a sorority or club because most of your friends or roommates are, but try to resist the temptation. Having friends around you in your various college activities can be a plus, but remember you are your own person and you want to be doing something you are truly happy doing. Besides, who knows, your friends might decide not to stick with it, you might follow suit, and that would leave the club with five or six empty seats that could have been filled with people who were more interested. And anyway, you'll feel better about your college experience if you have activities under your belt that are different from those of your friends. Remember, it's important to branch out. Do your own thing. You're the only one you have to please.

## You don't need to join an organization to make friends in college.

Eat in the cafeteria and strike up some conversations. Study at the library. Go to group study sessions. Keep the door open to your dorm room so people can drop by. If you're watching TV, invite people over to watch with you. Throw parties.

# the party scene

Parties are probably what you are looking forward to the most, and justifiably so. College parties can be fun and crazy, no doubt, or they can also be relaxing and chill. But, the one thing you can't avoid when it comes to partying is the presence of alcohol. It's important to mention that alcohol is illegal for those under twenty-one. It is a dangerous drug, as it impairs judgment and it can damage your body. However, it is a huge part of college life, whether or not you are twenty-one, so I will treat it as such in this chapter. It's important that you make your own decisions about alcohol. It *is* a part of college life in general, but it doesn't have to be a significant part of *your* life. No matter what you decide, you'll have fun regardless. It's pretty much impossible *not* to have a blast in college. Party *on*, girls.

It's amazing how many different ways and reasons college students have to celebrate. Here's a little preview of what types of parties you might encounter during these next four years. And, if you don't encounter any of these, that might be just enough incentive to throw a party yourself:

- **The toga party.** This tribute to ancient Greece is actually just an excuse to show a little bit of skin. Be discreet with this, ladies. The more skin you show, the more you might give the guys a certain impression about you. Be creative with your costume, and it's a great way to look sexy, no doubt. Just be prepared to ward off drunken guys drooling over your bare shoulder. Don't have an old sheet? Scope out the nearest thrift store. And try dressing up your costume with a gold belt. Be original and don't use a plain white sheet. Use bright colors and you'll turn some heads. And don't hesitate to crown yourself with laurel.
- **The Hawaiian luau.** Yup, yet another excuse to bare as much as possible. And a good time to sport your sexy bikini top. Don't forget to accessorize with flowers in your hair and a lei around your neck.
- **The frat party.** At these parties you'll probably spend most of your time pushing your way through the crowd to find the keg, and then waiting with an empty cup until the kegmaster chooses to fill it up. *Bring your own cup.* This could save time and money, as some of these parties run out of cups quickly, or charge a few bucks for a cup. Also,

you will most likely get spilled on. Wear sneakers or shoes that can handle beer spillage, and pull your hair back if you can to get it out of the way. Another thing: if you choose not to drink or to drink beforehand instead, it means you won't have to waste your time fighting the masses just for a cup of beer, and you'll have more time for socializing. Oh, and keep your guard up at these parties. The frat brothers tend to have an appetite for freshman girls, so don't fall victim to their charms too easily.

- **The dance party.** If you ask me, these parties are the most fun because they aren't so centered around alcohol. Hopefully these parties have good music to groove to. They might even have a real DJ. Be sure to wear a sexy, flashy outfit so you can attract a dance partner or two. Let yourself go; dance till your feet hurt ... it's great exercise, too!

## You don't have to drink to party in college.

People don't care about whether or not you drink. They care about whether or not you hang out and like to have fun.

- **The pre-party.** It's a party before you hit an actual party. This party serves several purposes. It provides a site for everyone in your crew to meet before hitting the scene. It's usually small and intimate, and includes cocktails or drinks of some sort. This eliminates the hassle of fighting the masses at the real party for something to drink. It's a great way to start the night. It's likely you will have an easier time talking to people at a pre-party, and this way you can ease into the night slowly.

- **The tailgate.** These parties are centered around sports events, such as football games. Students (and often alumni and local fans) get together for some food and beer to get excited for the game, but you don't have to be a sports fan to attend or enjoy the tailgate. Show some support for your team, though, if you feel moved to. These parties are the college version of high school pep rallies, but without all the cheesiness.

- **Drinking games.** Many parties are centered around drinking games, whether they be card games, beer pong, or games of other sorts. These can be fun and ridiculous, but they can also be an incredibly stupid way for people to drink in ways that are out of their control. **Know your limits.** Players of drinking games often have no mercy for the lightweights. Never drink more than you want to, and never let a jerk in a baseball cap tell you "the rules" say you have to take another drink.

- **The "chill" party.** At some parties people just get together to sit around, eat, drink, talk, listen to music. These parties are not so enjoyable for the socially inept, but if you hate the craziness of the other types of parties and prefer to just have some good conversation, this is the type of party to attend or host yourself.

## Throwing a party? A few tips to remember:

1. **Make some room.** Push furniture to the side and hide all valuables.
2. **Spill-proof your furniture.** Cover everything in garbage bags if you can. If not, stuff might get spilled on. On the other hand, you may not care about your secondhand couch, and if that's the case, don't even bother.
3. **Put out trashcans or garbage bags in visible places.**
4. **Make sure you have enough cups and lots of ice.**
5. **Music makes a big difference!** Have someone man the stereo system or play DJ for the night. Burn a few CDs of your favorite dance songs. Make sure the music is upbeat, so you can keep the energy of the party up.
6. **Provide some snacks.**
7. **Have someone play bartender.** If you're just going to have beer, no need to worry about this as much, but if you plan on providing mixed drinks, it's best to have someone man the alcohol. This way you won't have people sneaking away with your liquor.
8. **Post signs for the bathroom.** You don't want a confused partygoer mistaking the potted plant in your bedroom for a urinal.

## Some classic party tunes

- *All for Love*, Color Me Badd
- *Celebration*, Kool and the Gang
- *Baby Got Back*, Sir Mix-a-lot
- *Billie Jean*, Michael Jackson
- *Blister in the Sun*, Violent Femmes
- *Brick House*, The Commodores
- *Don't Worry Be Happy*, Bobby McFerrin
- *Gin and Juice*, Snoop Doggy Dogg
- *Girls Just Wanna Have Fun*, Cyndi Lauper
- *Good Vibrations*, Marky Mark
- *Hip Hop Hooray*, Naughty By Nature
- *Holiday*, Madonna
- *The Humpty Dance*, Digital Underground
- *I'm Too Sexy*, Right Said Fred
- *Informer*, Snow
- *I Wanna Sex You Up*, Color Me Badd
- *I Will Survive*, Gloria Gaynor
- *Jenny (867-5309)*, Tommy Tutone
- *Joy To The World*, Three Dog Night
- *Jump Around*, House of Pain
- *Jungle Boogie*, Kool and the Gang
- *Lady Marmalade*, Patti LaBelle
- *Like a Prayer*, Madonna
- *Like a Virgin*, Madonna

- *Love Rollercoaster*, Ohio Players
- *Material Girl*, Madonna
- *Motownphilly*, Boys II Men
- *My Sharona*, The Knack
- *Oh What a Night*, The Four Seasons
- *One Way or Another*, Blondie
- *O.P.P.*, Naughty By Nature
- *People Everyday*, Arrested Development
- *Play that Funky Music*, Wild Cherry
- *Rapper's Delight*, Sugar Hill Gang
- *Rock & Roll All Night*, Kiss
- *Rump Shaker*, Wreckx-N-Effect
- *Smooth Criminal*, Michael Jackson
- *Summertime*, DJ Jazzy Jeff and the Fresh Prince
- *The Sweater Song*, Weezer
- *Sweet Home Alabama*, Lynyrd Skynyrd
- *Tainted Love*, Soft Cell
- *Thriller*, Michael Jackson
- *Walking On Sunshine*, Katrina & The Waves
- *Walk Like An Egyptian*, The Bangles
- *Whip It*, Devo
- *Wild Thing*, Tone Loc
- *You Spin Me Round*, Dead or Alive

# handling your alcohol

If you choose to drink in college, it's important that you know how to take control of yourself when it comes to alcohol consumption. Drinking can be fun, but it can also be unsafe. Obviously the safest thing to do is not drink at all (and just make fun of everyone else acting stupid while drunk), but if you choose to, keep the following things in mind.

**Know your limits.** It may take a while to figure out how much alcohol you can handle, but the general rules are: *a) the smaller you are, the lower your tolerance, b) the more often you drink, the higher your tolerance, and c) the less food you have in your stomach, the faster you get drunk.* Just get to know yourself and how much you can drink before what you drank comes back up. Stop drinking when your stomach starts to feel queasy, or better yet, when you feel really good and aren't quite drunk yet. You don't have to be completely wasted to have fun. Just be smart about it.

**Look out for your friends, and have them look out for you.** Who knows what will happen if you've had too much to drink, so it's important you have someone lucid around to keep you and your friends from doing anything stupid or dangerous, or at least to hold your hair back when you are hunched over the toilet. And **DON'T DRIVE DRUNK, OR LET ANYONE ELSE DO SO.**

> **"Beer before liquor, never been sicker; liquor before beer, you're in the clear."**
>
> For most people, including me, this saying holds true. For others, it doesn't mean a thing. In general, it's not a good idea to mix it up, no matter what the order is.

**Water, water, everywhere.** Water is the best cure for all problems relating to too much alcohol. Alcohol dehydrates your body, so if ever you start to feel sick, you know you need some hydration. Drink water right after a night of drinking, and also right after puking, if you get sick. Leave a glass of water right by your bed or by the door so you can grab it and down it before you hit the sack. And don't chug the water, just sip it. Other options are Alka-Seltzer, ginger ale, saltine crackers, and bread.

## Know what you're drinking.

We've all heard horror stories about date-rape drugs being slipped into drinks. Don't let it happen to you. Never drink something that was just handed to you by someone you don't know and trust. Pour and mix your drinks yourself so you know what goes into them and where they come from. And refrain from drinking any kind of mystery punch. If you are sleepy or drowsy, find a friend and go home immediately.

**Know your resources for help in situations like these.** Keep phone numbers in your wallet of an on-campus escort service, your RA, a minibus, or an emergency contact.

**If you are with someone who starts to puke, make sure they stay upright and conscious.** If they pass out or are in an awkward position, they could choke. Make sure they drink water, and don't leave them by themselves. If they really look severely sick, or are starting to pass out, GET HELP. Horrible as it is to think about, there have been a few widely publicized cases in the last few years of college students dying from alcohol-related accidents. Don't think twice about taking your friend to the hospital—emergency rooms are used to seeing students in this state, and you might save a life.

**Handle a hangover with water, a pain reliever, and some greasy food.** If you wake up with a hangover, there's not much you can do but suffer through it. To feel better, take some ibuprofen, drink more water, and eat some greasy food, which will absorb the alcohol in your stomach.

## Don't drink if you are on prescription medication.

Combining drugs (your medication and the alcohol) could really screw up your system, and even kill you.

# chapter nine

# guys and sex: the college dating scene

**a**h, the chapter you've been waiting for. I bet you are pretty much fed up with high school boys by now, and rightfully so. You probably grew up with most of them, witnessing *all* of it—nose-picking, pimples, braces, squeaking voices—and somehow they have lost their charm. It's time for a new batch of guys to choose from, and college is the perfect place to find not boys, but men. Well, not really *men* quite yet, but closer to that sort than high school boys will ever be, and therefore much more worthy of your time and energy. Take advantage of this opportunity, girls. At no other point in your life will you be able to sample the personalities of guys from all different walks of life, many of whom will be just as interested in getting to know you as you are interested in them. In these next four years you might meet the man of your dreams. They say many of us meet our future mates in college, even if it's just in passing. Many college sweethearts end up married soon after college, and others who were merely acquaintances in college discover years later that they were meant to be together. Take note of every guy you encounter because even if he doesn't have potential now, he may later. Don't be frenzied by your search for a soulmate, however. That kind of thing happens on its own. Take advantage of this chance to meet as many guys as you can. You won't have many opportunities like this later on in life.

One thing to note: **freshman guys, for the most part, only have two things in mind, beer and sex.** Regardless of what they say or do to convince you otherwise, the underlying motivation for all of their actions are these two things. Freshman boys will undoubtedly be the bane of your existence during your first year at college. They are having doors opened for them that were dead-bolted shut in high school. Like hungry dogs, they are twitching with anticipation of the sexual opportunities the pains of being at home prevented them from having. To them, college is the perfect site for finally satisfying their carnal desires. And we can say beer is essentially their fuel, or secondary impetus, for achieving their first: sex. **Beer is an excuse and also a relaxant. It erases inhibitions and somehow justifies otherwise off-the-wall behavior.**

This isn't to say that we girls aren't also excited to have opportunities presented to us as we enter college. These are the only four years of your life when you will be thrown together with thousands of similarly sexually driven people in a completely new place suffused with constant energy and the thrill of discovery (and lacking in parental control). The situation begs to be taken advantage of—and most people do just that. In my years at school I've seen naked classmates running through dorms handing out candy during exam time. I've been to a naked party or two, and I have witnessed some nasty business going on in the stacks in the library. No doubt, women are curious about sex, too, but we have those little impediments called emotions that don't allow us as much guiltless freedom as guys seem to have.

When you're dealing with guys in college, you always seem to be dealing with sex, too. The two things are pretty much interchangeable. No matter how you plan on approaching problems when it comes to guys and sex, **NEVER FORGET** three things:

1. **Be safe and protected.** As a college student, the last thing you need is to get unexpectedly pregnant or to contract a sexually transmitted disease (STD). *Learn about the different methods of contraception, and use them.*

2. **A reputation is easy to gain and hard to lose.** You don't want to live the rest of your years at college with "slut" attached to your name. *Respect yourself.*

3. **Don't let yourself be taken advantage of.** How do you know if you are being taken advantage of? If beer is involved, you are. If sex is involved way too soon, you are. But sometimes it isn't that simple. Remember their two motives. (One starts with a *b* and the other with an *s*, if you somehow forgot.) Those two motives lie behind many of their actions.

He may make you feel like a confidante, someone "not like the other girls." He may gain your trust by making you feel special, and then make the moves on you later. *Keep your guard up.*

If you keep these things in mind when confronted with your dilemmas, you will be on your way to making the right decisions.

# dating

College is the perfect time and place for dating. Actually, dating in college is quite different from dating in any other environment—so different that it might seem like you aren't dating at all. But believe it or not, as you meet more guys and start to hang out with them, you ARE dating. Sure, there may not be an official exchange of phone numbers, a shy phone call asking you out, a nervous greeting at the door with flowers in hand, an awkward night of dinner and a movie, followed by a clumsy kiss at the doorstep. It just doesn't happen that way. More likely than not, you'll meet someone offhand at a party or through an activity, and somehow you will encounter each other more and more, until you work up the initiative to plan these encounters and eventually hang out on a regular basis. It sort of occurs without you even knowing it and, if you ask me, that's what's so great about it.

Dating, or really, *hanging out*, is the best way to get to know guys in college. You'll have the most fun, and you'll get to know the most guys. It's remarkable how many different types of guys the college environment seems to breed. The tricky part is figuring out which guy is right for you.

## College guy types (and how to spot them)

*The Alpha Kappa Greek Dude* (aka Frat Boy)

**The look:** Baseball cap, khakis, the semi-annual "frat party" T-shirt.

**Where to find him:** At the frat house doing pledge chores, or, if he's a "brother," watching ESPN or *Girls Gone Wild* while being waited on hand and foot by pledges.

**First date:** Date? Just come to this Friday's frat party after the first beer pong game, but before he's completely drunk.

**Beverage of choice:** Cheap beer from a keg in a red plastic cup.

**Why would you date him?** You miss high school, or you miss baby-sitting.

*The Super-Star Athlete* (aka Jock)

**The look:** T-shirt, athletic shorts and sweats with school logo.

**Where to find him:** At the gym, at his games, or on the quad playing sports (hopefully with his shirt off).

**First date:** A sports bar. Forget the sexy mini-dress, just wear jeans.

**Beverage of choice:** Sports drinks found in the glass refrigerator at the gym, or beer by the pitcher.

**Why would you date him?** You've always been confused by sports and want to "learn." You like his body. You're not really into conversation.

*The Dramatist* (aka That Artsy Guy)

**The look:** Black, black, turtlenecks, black.

**Where to find him:** In smoky coffee shops and bars, reading scripts and smoking cigarettes. He'll be the one in black.

**First date:** Watching that new foreign film or Sundance second runner-up.

**Beverage of choice:** Coffee—BLACK.

**Why would you date him?** You want depth and poetry in your life. You like black. When you're older and see him in the new AT&T commercial, you can say, "I dated him!"

*The Musician* (aka Rock Star)

**The look:** Ripped jeans, concert shirts.

**Where to find him:** At local bars playing cool covers of the Red Hot Chili Peppers and Aerosmith.

**First date:** A concert, of course.

**Beverage of choice:** Whatever his fans buy him between sets or what the bartender hooks him up with.

**Why would you date him?** Doesn't *every* girl want to date someone in a band??

*The Computer Nerd* (aka Boy Version 6.0b)

**The look:** Old T-shirts, jeans.

**Where to find him:** At the computer lab or in his room in front of his computer.

**First date:** Internet chat room—screen name: "GandalfRulz"—meet him there.

**Beverage of choice:** Anything with lots of caffeine, preferably carbonated (it's hard to keep staring at that computer screen).

**Why would you date him?** To get your computer fixed, or because he could be the future Bill Gates.

*Mr. Perfect* (aka The Player)

**The look:** Whatever he wants—vintage, retro—guys make fun of him, but girls find his style a sign of "confidence."

**Where to find him:** Wherever girls are that regular guys are afraid to venture—coffee shops, artsy bars, bookstores, museums.

**First date:** A cool restaurant or funky location where you will be impressed and romanced, maybe a moonlight picnic by the lake near campus, or the hot new club where he has VIP entrance.

**Beverage of choice:** Red wine (a good year) or cocktails (shaken, not stirred).

**Why would you date him?** Because you don't know better, because
he says, "You're not like other girls …
you're different, you're special."

*The Foreign Guy* (aka Euro)
**The look:** Straight out of *GQ*; his clothes actually fit (and match!),
though they are sometimes too tight.
**Where to find him:** At places regular college students can't
afford—nice restaurants, the opera, trendy
bars for the mid-twenties crowd.
**First date:** A good restaurant with an excellent wine selection.
**Beverage of choice:** Perrier, a good espresso, or a fine bottle of
wine.
**Why would you date him?** You're doing your part to get to know
other cultures. It's a small world after
all. And besides, you're bored of
regular old Americans.

*The Prep* (aka College MAN)
**The look:** Clean, ironed, name brand clothes
**Where to find him:** At the career center, or involved in the latest
campus activity. You know those events
advertised on those flyers you see up all
around campus? Yup, he's there.
**First date:** A semi-formal campus or alumni event. Have a cocktail
dress and high heels on hand, and get ready to mingle.
**Beverage of choice:** Micro brews, bottled beer—sometimes
imported.
**Why would you date him?** Guilt—this is who your parents would
have wanted … they are spending so
much money, it's the least you could
do; because you want more uses out
of your prom dress.

**Does dating really exist in college?** *"I hung out with this guy at a party, and we totally hit it off and spent all night talking. He walked me home and we sat outside talking until 6 a.m., and then he came up to my room and we talked for even longer ... and then he finally kissed me, and it was all sweet and comfortable. He e-mailed me a few days later and asked me out, and we went out for coffee. A couple days later I got this voicemail from him, all panicky and just plain weird, saying how he 'can't be in a relationship, it's just too much for him at this point, he is feeling all overwhelmed with everything.' Whoa, there, buddy. What relationship? We were just supposed to be getting to know each other better. I hate it when boys are so confusing. I immediately e-mailed him and said no worries, it's all cool ... but it wasn't, really. We were pretty awkward around each other after that, which is lame and sad. I learned a couple of lessons from that one: 1) It's impossible to casually date someone in college. There's just no such thing as two people who just want to get to know each other better. For some stupid reason, it always has to be all or nothing. 2) Just because a boy seems dorky and vulnerable and harmless, does not mean that he can't hurt you."*

– Erica Kaye, Bethesda, Maryland

If you start to become interested in someone, remember these tips:
1. **Be yourself!** You'll be the most comfortable getting to know a guy if you act naturally. And believe me, no matter who you are trying to be, the real you is more attractive to any guy rather than a fake anybody.

2. **Be confident.** Don't be too eager, but don't shrink away either. You'll scare the guy away by being in his face all the time, but it won't do any good to make no effort at all. Just casually ask him to hang out. You've got nothing to lose.

> **College is filled with events and activities perfect for a date.**
>
> Go to a concert, play, or musical. Go rollerblading. Rent videos and order pizza in your dorm room. Go to a sports event. Visit a tourist attraction in the city your school is in. Go to a nightclub or bar. Have a picnic at a local park. Go to dinner and a movie. Go out for coffee. Talk until sunrise on the rooftop of a tall building. Go bowling. Visit a museum. Work out together. Play one-on-one hoops. Play poker or another card game. Sing karaoke at a bar. Go to a campus party. Attend a dance.

3. **Don't take things too seriously.** Remember all you're trying to do is get to know the guy, or a few guys for that matter. It's not as though you are looking for your future husband, so don't read into things, and don't overanalyze. Just have fun getting to know him. Things tend to get serious really fast in college, much faster than they should. Go slow.

4. **Don't let him get under your skin.** Don't fill your time wondering if he likes you, what he's doing, when he's going to call. No guy is worth all that mental energy. The point of dating is that you get to hang out with guys and have fun without having to think about them all the time. And, if he turns out to be a jerk, he isn't worth your time. Remember you're just perusing, so if you've discovered a dud, get over it and move on. There are so many other guys to meet; it's not worth letting one ruin your college experience, or even ruin your week. It's pretty much impossible to avoid the jerks, so you might as well accept that from the beginning.

5. **Go with the flow.** Don't have any expectations. That way, you can't get disappointed. Even if things are going well, and a relationship seems to be on the horizon, don't expect it. You might be wrong. Don't expect guys in college to be your knights in shining armor. Most of the time

they have no idea how to communicate, how to treat women, or how to be human beings in general. It's sad, but very true. (Still, for what it's worth, they're about fifty times better than the best high school boy.)

**The bottom line on dating:**

Have fun! This is the best way to make the most out of college.

# the random hookup

In college there is an entirely new type of interaction between girls and guys that is most commonly known as the **random hookup.** In this situation, a girl and a guy theoretically get together with the sole purpose of enjoying some physical interaction, however large or small, with no strings attached. The two involved may be friends, they may be acquaintances, or they may be total strangers. Regardless of the nature of their relationship, the point of the interaction is to get some *play.*

Not surprisingly, these random hookups occur more often in college than they probably should. It's just too easy. You're both horny and curious, you've got no one to answer to, and neither of you are looking for anything more than a little bit of sinful pleasure, without the hassle of a relationship.

Well, it may depend on the type of person you are, but for most of us, **the random hookup turns out to be more of a problem than anything else.** Not only are you putting yourself at risk for STDs by engaging in casual sexual activity, you also shouldn't forget about those impediments that I mentioned earlier that are otherwise known to us as *emotions.* **Once you get physical with a guy, it's really hard not to get emotionally attached.** After all, as cheesy as it sounds, our bodies are sacred to us, and once we allow someone to cross that threshold, we can't help but feel as though we deserve more than just physical benefits.

Let's put things in perspective. Once you've experienced a random hookup, one of the following will result:

> "It's generally best not to read anything into a random hookup since that's just what it is, a random hookup! If the interest keeps, you'll know, but not expecting it either way will help prevent a lot of confusion and hurt feelings. And always always ALWAYS use birth control! Or else, don't have sex. It's really very simple."
> – Alice Ko, Diamond Bar, California

1. **Thanks, and see ya never.** You forget about him, no discomfort, no regrets.

     This result seems ideal, doesn't it? Well, unfortunately, first of all, it's rare, and second of all, even if you're lucky enough to have no regrets, this outcome is not so ideal for your reputation and self-respect. The more comfortable you are with hooking up with any guy, the more often you will do it. The more random guys you hook up with, the more at risk you are for pregnancy and STDs. Even if you are not having intercourse, you are always still at risk. Also, REMEMBER: **Word travels fast and you could gain a reputation that you don't want to have.** You might become known as *easy* or even worse, a *slut*. Or, one of your partners may fall head over heels for you, and you could break his heart. There's nothing wrong with sexual experimentation, but you can experiment without being careless. **Be selective of your partners, and although it's just experimentation, it is also sex, and sex should be taken seriously.**

2. **Thanks, and see ya tomorrow?** You are *so* okay with what you did, that you hook up with him again, and *again*. No emotional attachment, just a new, um, "play"-mate.

     Well then, you think, outcome number *two* is the ideal one, isn't it? Um, not so much. True, it seems that way because two people are getting the action they want, without the baggage. You aren't disrespecting yourself or your body by having multiple partners, but instead you are having a monogamous sexual relationship. The thing is, **the more sexually involved you get, the closer you get to becoming emotionally attached.** And it's likely that even though one person (you, perhaps) lets their emotions take effect, the other person won't feel the same way. Now, if the feelings are mutual, this could be a good thing. However, in my experience, relationships based on sex almost always fail. So, **if you plan on pursuing a legit, serious relationship with a hookup, try to lay off the physical stuff for a while and let the relationship develop the right way.**

---

**The walk of shame.** *"This is the walk from his room to yours the next morning, post-hookup. Everyone has done it at some point. It never becomes less embarrassing. I remember one that was particularly bad, mostly because my skimpy red dress and black stiletto heels did not help me fit in with the early Sunday morning church crowd. Moral: make him lend you a T-shirt. He owes you more than that anyway."*

– Lisa Javier, New York City, New York

---

3. **What did I just DO??** You feel uncomfortable with what you did, and you regret it.

It's okay to feel uncomfortable and regretful of a random hookup. In most cases, you probably wouldn't have hooked up with the guy if the situation had been different. Whatever the case, just learn from the experience, and realize that **the fact that you regret it means that you just aren't cut out for casual sex.** *And that's a good thing.* Remember also that it's okay to make mistakes. You may have done something you regret, but at least you learn from it. And the fact is, a *lot* of girls in college make the same mistake. So you're not alone. Talk to your girlfriends (or better yet, an older sister) about it. Tell them how you feel. It will help you understand the experience and you will feel reassured that you're not the only one.

4. **The pangs of unrequited love.** You start to like the guy, but he couldn't care less about you, or vice versa.

Now if after this one hookup, one of you gets attached and the other just wants to move on, someone's heart could get broken. If you're the one who can't get him out of your head, and it's fairly obvious that it was just a one-night stand to him, I wouldn't recommend pursuing a relationship him. He probably won't give in, and, if he does, it's likely that he's only in it for the sex. Besides, the healthiest relationships don't begin with a one-night stand. On the other hand, if he's the one who wants to pursue a relationship, and you're not interested, just be straight with him from the beginning. Let him down easy, but don't lead him on. Sure, you might break his heart, but hey, that's life.

---

**Tell him where you draw the line, even if it kills the mood.** *"So we're sitting on his bed, just kissing, nothing huge, when all of a sudden he bolts up and stammers, 'I have to go to the bathroom, I'll be right back,' and he hurriedly exits the room. I'm sitting there, waiting for him to come back, and it's dawning on me that going home with a perfect stranger was possibly not the smartest thing I've ever done, considering I didn't know anything about this boy! I started thinking maybe I should be heading home, not lying on this random guy's bed, when he suddenly returns to the room. In one quick movement, he strips off his shirt and hits the lights—and now it's pitch-black and there's this half-naked guy I don't know at all, all over me. I guess I just panicked because I suddenly blurted, 'NO SEX!' Yeah, that killed the mood. Fortunately, in the end it turned out fine, 'cause he was all sweet and actually a virgin himself, and it was one of the nicer hookups I've ever experienced."*
                                            – Carmen Jimenez, San Juan, Puerto

---

**5. A romance blossoms.** You start to like the guy, and he starts to like you, too.

If both of you are sincerely into each other, by all means, let the romance begin. However, as I said in number two, **if you plan on pursuing a legit, serious relationship, lay off the physical stuff for a while and let the relationship develop the right way.** If sex is a major part of the relationship from the start, it isn't healthy, and the relationship is bound to end sooner rather than later. And, believe me, it won't be a happy ending. The healthiest relationships begin with two people really getting to know each other and becoming comfortable with each other. You have to take the time to evaluate whether or not you click well enough to get seriously involved. A serious relationship takes time and energy, and it's *not easy*. It's not worth the effort if you find that you can't even have a real conversation with the guy.

## The bottom line on the random hookup:

Just don't do it. It's not worth it in the long run.

# getting serious

If you are looking for a serious relationship as soon as you get to college (which I don't recommend), don't set your sights on boys your age, as in: **AVOID FRESHMAN BOYS.** Look higher, at upperclassmen who have gotten the wildness out of their system and who have begun to take control of their lives and finally care about their academics and their future—a **guy who can't even control his hormones certainly won't be able to handle a relationship.**

But, don't look for a serious relationship your freshman year. Use this year as a time to get to know yourself and other people in this new environment. It's like window-shopping. Peruse the merchandise, and figure out what you will want when you finally make a purchase later. If you get to know enough guys (safely, *platonically*), you'll know what types of guys are out there for you to choose from, and you'll be able to piece together in your mind the type of guy you'll eventually want to end up with. By keeping an open mind and not committing yourself, while still having fun meeting people, you'll be able to make an educated decision later when the possibility of a relationship arises.

Besides, **freshman year is a time of exploration.** A serious relationship hinders your opportunities to see who and what is out there. Freshman year is when you find your niche and discover the people that you will be hanging out with and bonding with for the rest of your years at college. And these people will be your family away from home. Committing yourself to one person right off the bat could mean that you will have very few people to turn to later.

In any case, a serious relationship isn't something anyone should really be actively looking for. **The best relationships happen by accident.** Don't let the search for a soul mate define your college experience. Just have fun and take care of yourself. Do whatever makes you happy. Surround yourself with people you have fun with. If the opportunity for a relationship somehow arises, great. Go for it. If not, it doesn't matter, because you're having a blast anyway!

Now, if you do happen to fall into a serious relationship, hopefully it will happen later on in college, say your junior year, when you're probably more prepared to get serious. Make sure you know what you're getting into. Relationships are difficult to maintain already, and even more so in college. They require a lot of time and emotional energy, and in order to make them work, you have to be able to trust and be trusted, and be willing to communicate.

**DON'T let the relationship consume you.** As much as you might be in love, don't make him your entire life. As my older sister said to me when I was in a serious relationship, "You may be flying high, but don't forget your friends and family. They are the ones who keep you grounded." Maintain a good balance between him and the other people in your life. The relationship may not last, and if it doesn't, you don't want your world to fall apart.

> **Never get involved (either emotionally or physically) with a guy who has a dependency on drugs or alcohol.**
>
> Alcoholics and drug addicts can do nothing less than cause you pain in the long run.

**Be patient and listen.** Relationships are not just based on attraction and infatuation, but also on communicating, trusting, and understanding each other. This kind of strong connection between two people might take a while to build. Make an effort to listen to him, and to understand who he is and what he needs; expect him to do the same for you.

**Your happiness should come from yourself, not from him.** *Don't forget your independence.* It's okay to lean on him once in a while, but don't become dependent on him, nor should he become dependent on you. As my mom says, a relationship should be "a union of strength." You and your boyfriend should be independent, secure, and happy with yourselves as individuals first and foremost, rather than depending on each other for personal happiness and security. If you're confident and feel good about who you are, and if he feels the same way about himself, your relationship will be far more likely to last.

**Relationships are tough, so it's okay if you decide that you're not ready.** This is a crazy time in your life. You are going through a lot of changes, and you probably still haven't gotten to know yourself well enough to become really comfortable with who you are as an individual. Not only that, you've got to handle classes, think about your career, and learn to take care of yourself all at once. It's hard to do all of that and be a good girlfriend at the same time. If you find that it's just too much to deal with, get out of the relationship. It might be painful, but you'll be doing both of you a favor in the long run. You might feel so in love you believe you are meant for each other, but this doesn't mean it's right for you to be together now. If you really are meant to be, you'll be.

### The bottom line on getting serious:

Don't look for it; let it happen. And if it does, know that a relationship entails a lot time and energy. Don't get serious if you aren't ready; you've got to be comfortable with yourself first. Be loving, patient, and always communicate.

# sex

It's pretty tough to avoid sex in college. That doesn't mean actually *having sex*, because *that* you *can* avoid if you choose to. But, sex as an issue is pretty much inevitable. Even if you choose not to bother with it, you'll probably have to deal with guys who want it from you, or friends who will need your support and advice when they are trying to deal with all of its accompanying problems and confusions. This is why it's important to educate yourself. This means getting to know and becoming comfortable with your body, and learning about and using methods of contraception and protection to prevent pregnancy and STDs.

> **Don't think you need to decide whether to date or whether to have a serious boyfriend.** *"Take care of yourself, have fun. Dates and serious boyfriends sometimes happen, sometimes not."*
>
> – Alice Ko, Diamond Bar, California

**Get to know your body.** The more familiar you are with your body, the more comfortable you will be in confronting sex. You may feel kind of strange at first, and this is because traditionally we haven't been encouraged to get to know our bodies. Well, fortunately, times have changed. It's important to take the time to learn about your sexual and reproductive organs and about your own menstrual cycle. The more you know, the better you will be able to take care of your body both for your everyday experiences and when sex is involved.

**Visit your gynecologist once a year.** By the time you enter college you should have already had your first gynecological examination. If not, schedule one soon. The gynecologist's office is a good place to start learning about your body, and it's important to visit annually to make sure you are healthy. Become familiar with your reproductive system by watching and understanding what happens during your examination. Your doctor will perform an external and internal pelvic exam, as well as a Pap Smear, which is a screening test for cervical cancer. In addition to this test, you may also ask your doctor to test you for any STDs or pregnancy. Your doctor will also examine your breasts for breast cancer, and teach you how to perform a breast self-exam, which you should perform once a month.

**Keep track of your menstrual cycle.** Start recording on a calendar when you get your period, if you don't already. Once you start keeping track, you'll be able figure out when you can blame acne breakouts or crankiness on PMS, and you'll also be able to determine more positively if your period is late and if you could be pregnant.

**Use contraception.** It's probably been drilled into your head since middle school, but it can never be said enough. If you're going to have sex, do it safely. Use contraception to protect yourself from getting pregnant or contracting STDs. When making a decision on which contraceptive to use it's important to weigh the advantages and disadvantages of each, and consider which one is right for your needs. Most college students tend to use either the condom or the pill, both of which require minimal in-the-moment hassle, and seem to be more fitting for the college lifestyle. If you choose to take the pill, keep in mind that what you will essentially be controlling your hormones, and this can often have negative side effects. It's also important to note that there isn't just one type of pill, but rather many different kinds, with different dosages. The pill is convenient and highly effective, but it also takes a while for your body to adjust to it, and it might take a while to figure out which one is right for your body. The condom and the pill, however, are not your only options. Other possibilities include the female condom, diaphragm, cervical cap, as well as spermicide, Norplant, an intrauterine device, and Depo-Provera. All have their strengths and weaknesses. It's best to talk to your doctor about your choices.

**Learn about sexually transmitted diseases.** As effective as methods of contraception may be, none of them are absolutely guaranteed to protect you against STDs, so you need to be aware no matter what. And, as is often the case with sex, you may not have the forethought in the heat of passion to be as careful as you should be, so it's important to watch out for what may be symptoms of STDs. In general, if you experience any of the following symptoms in the genital area, you should see your gynecologist or health practitioner as soon as possible:

*abnormal or smelly discharges, bleeding, blisters, boils, buboes (swollen lymph node in the groin), burning sensations, cervicitis (inflamed cervix), chancres (sores or ulcers), growths, irritations, itches, odors, painful intercourse, pains, polyps, pus, rashes, sores, swellings, tenderness, ulcers, urine changes, vaginal yeast infections, warts*

As for the symptoms of specific sexually transmitted diseases, it's best to talk to a health professional.

# pregnancy

Despite all the available methods of contraception, there is no absolute guarantee that you won't get pregnant, unless you remain abstinent. If you miss a period and suspect you might be pregnant, it may be time to take a test. Anxiety and impatience (understandably) will have you rushing to the twenty-four-hour drugstore for a test you can administer privately as soon as possible. Just don't rely solely on the result of a drugstore test. Go to a clinic and have the test administered by a doctor or nurse as soon as you can make an appointment. Whatever the results, the doctor or nurse who administers the test will be able to give you more information on your options and what you can do.

Remember that your body is your temple, and you must take precious care of it. *"Being safe and taking responsibilities for your actions doesn't mean you can't have fun, but it does mean you should think carefully about what you do and how you do it. One mistake I think a lot of college women make is to believe (somewhat falsely) that if they know a guy, or their friends know him, then he is automatically 'safe' territory, i.e., he probably doesn't have any diseases or any terrible past history. But believe me, just because a guy goes to an Ivy League school or comes from a well-known family does NOT mean that he is any more 'clean' than any other guy you will meet. Even if you have been dating someone for six months or are in love with them or think you know them inside and out, you still need to protect your body and your health. With every guy that I've ever been sexually involved with, I have always made him get tested for STDs and AIDS (and in turn I have agreed to be tested, too). If you get nervous about asking a guy to do this, just remember, if he has a problem with it, he's not man enough for you. And there have been times when the guy has sort of looked at me in shock, and assured me that he's totally fine—and I believe him—but I still like to have confirmation that I am not going to put myself at risk. Even if you use a condom, it can break. If you're on birth control, you aren't protected from STDs at all. So call it what you will—neurotic, obsessive, whatever. But I'm going to be the girl who has fun and doesn't get hurt. All it takes is a little extra bit of vigilance and the self-confidence to say that you (and your body) are worth the slight inconvenience of taking a blood test."*

– Annie Fishman, Boston, Massachusetts

a girl's guide (abridged)

# 21 rules for making the most of college

1. Get to know yourself and become comfortable with who you are.
2. Be independent and responsible.
3. Take care of and respect yourself: emotionally, mentally, and physically.
4. Don't stress out.
5. Embrace change; it's inevitable.
6. Explore. Experiment. Investigate.
7. Always have clean underwear.
8. Be open-minded.
9. Get to know as many people as you can and allow people to get to know you.
10. Get some sleep.
11. Persevere in everything you do.
12. Be safe.
13. Save up some money for a rainy day.
14. Challenge yourself.
15. Learn not just from your classes, but also from experience, and from the people around you.
16. Throw a party at least once.
17. Pursue your interests.
18. Try something new.
19. Appreciate every person, opportunity, and obstacle that comes your way.
20. Change for the better.
21. Have fun!

# looking back at four irreplaceable years

**e**very college girl's experience is unique, but we can also learn from each other, gaining and dispensing the wisdom that only experience can offer. No matter what happens, your four years of college are going to be irreplaceable, and you'll wish you could live them over and over again. Somehow it seems impossible to fit everything you want to do into just four years. You'll wish college were twice as long, just so you could have the chance to try everything.

Live life to the fullest while you're there—*carpe diem*, as they say. Seize the day while you've got the time to do so. College is filled with opportunities that you may never have once you graduate. That's not to say life ends after college, but at no other time in your life will you get a chance to preview and sample every possible activity, personality, and relationship that exists in the real world.

The day you graduate, you'll be leaving with the best four years of your life in your pocket. You want to be able to reflect on those four years without regret, and with appreciation that you were able to come away learning so much about yourself and the people around you. Every year of college will find you changing, and always for the better. You'll grow as a person and as a woman, and with the start of each year, you'll look back on the previous one in awe of how much your attitude and perhaps even your view of the world has changed.

College is your preparation for the real world, not just intellectually. You learn the most not from your professors, but from the people you meet and the experiences you have outside of the classroom. Don't underestimate the value of the people around you. Get to know as many people as you can, and appreciate their idiosyncrasies and every story they have to tell.

Enjoy the uncertainty that characterizes college life because after these four years you'll have to make decisions and start moving in some sort of definitive direction. And while you're drifting, keep your eyes peeled for something you feel passionate about.

You'll know you've made the most of college if, in the end, you've changed for the better, made some great friends, and learned a thing or two about life.

No matter what, have *fun*, girls. Come to think of it, it may be difficult *not* to.

# acknowledgements

**a**s much as I'd like to take full credit for the creation of this book, I can't. There are many people I have to thank for helping me to ensure that *a girl's guide to college* reached its full potential. Thanks to the real-life college girls who shared their advice and stories: Joy Chia, Hilary McQuaide, Lindsay Tracy, Sarah Chihaya, Alice Ko, Erica Kaye, Annie Fishman, Arija Weddle, Emily Di Capua, and Ann Moller. Thanks to all the women of Something Extra, whose examples I learned from throughout my four years of college; you are all quite an inspiring group of college women. Also thanks to Mike Doran, John Goeltz, Miye Moriguchi, Ann, Arija, and Lindsay for their meticulous copyediting and suggestions. And thanks to my family: my mom, Tina, and my sister, Tanya, without whose love, guidance and advice I wouldn't have survived college; and my dad, Ben, and my brother, Raul, and Daniel, for their love and support. A huge thanks to Josh Lambert, the best and most supportive editor a first-time author could possibly ask for, and also to my sister Tanya, whose artistic and creative contributions are present from cover to cover. And, I can't forget to thank everyone at SPS Studios for their encouragement right from the beginning. I couldn't have done it without all of you. Thanks!

# index

# about the author

**t**raci maynigo has just survived the best four years of her life at Yale University ('03), and graduated as an English major. During her years in college, she spent most of her time singing in an a cappella group, grooving at dance parties, editing a literary magazine, writing for fun, and becoming utterly confused by college guys. When at home in Washington, D.C., she may be found shopping in Georgetown, hitting the club scene, or watching live concerts. Now that she's graduated, she roams the streets of New York City, a fearless member of the dreaded post-college real world, reminiscing about college.